Jazz

Lucent Library of Black History

Ronald D. Lankford, Jr.

LUCENT BOOKS
A part of Gale, Cengage Learning

GALE
CENGAGE Learning

Detroit • New York • San Francisco • New Haven, Conn • Waterville, Maine • London

LIBRARY OF CONGRESS CATALOGING-IN-PUBLICATION DATA

Lankford, Ronald D., 1962-
Jazz / by Ronald D. Lankford, Jr.
  p. cm. -- (Lucent library of black history)
Includes bibliographical references and index.
ISBN 978-1-4205-0570-2 (hardcover)
1. Jazz--History and criticism. 2. African Americans--Music--History and criticism. I. Title.
ML3508.L38 2011
781.6509--dc22

2011002417

Lucent Books
27500 Drake Rd.
Farmington Hills, MI 48331

ISBN-13: 978-1-4205-0570-2
ISBN-10: 1-4205-0570-X

Printed in the United States of America
1 2 3 4 5 6 7 15 14 13 12 11

Printed by Bang Printing, Brainerd, MN, 1st Ptg., 04/2011

Contents

Foreword

It has been more than 500 years since Africans were first brought to the New World in shackles, and over 140 years since slavery was formally abolished in the United States. Over 50 years have passed since the fallacy of "separate but equal" was obliterated in the American courts, and some 40 years since the watershed Civil Rights Act of 1965 guaranteed the rights and liberties of all Americans, especially those of color. Over time, these changes have become celebrated landmarks in American history. In the twenty-first century, African American men and women are politicians, judges, diplomats, professors, deans, doctors, artists, athletes, business owners, and home owners. For many, the scars of the past have melted away in the opportunities that have been found in contemporary society. Observers such as Peter N. Kirsanow, who sits on the U.S. Commission of Civil Rights, point to these accomplishments and conclude, "The growing black middle class may be viewed as proof that most of the civil rights battles have been won."

In spite of these legal victories, however, prejudice and inequality have persisted in American society. In 2003, African Americans comprised just 12 percent of the nation's population, yet accounted for 44 percent of its prison inmates and 24 percent of its poor. Racially motivated hate crimes continue to appear on the pages of major newspapers in many American cities. Furthermore, many African Americans still experience either overt or muted racism in their daily lives. A 1996 study undertaken by Professor Nancy Krieger of the Harvard School of Public Health, for example, found that 80 percent of the African American participants reported having experienced racial discrimination in one or more settings, including at work or school, applying for housing and medical care, from the police or in the courts, and on the street or in a public setting.

It is for these reasons that many believe the struggle for racial equality and justice is far from over. These episodes of discrimination threaten to shatter the illusion that America has completely overcome its racist past, causing many black Americans to become increasingly frustrated and confused. Scholar and writer Ellis Cose has described this splintered state in the following way: "I have done everything I was supposed to do. I have stayed out of trouble with the law, gone to the right schools, and worked myself nearly to death. What more do they want? Why in God's name won't they accept me as a full human being?" For Cose and others, the struggle for equality and justice has yet to be fully achieved.

In many subtle yet important ways the traumatic experiences of slavery and segregation continue to inform the way race is discussed and experienced in the twenty-first century. Indeed, it is possible that America will always grapple with the fallout from its distressing past. Ulric Haynes, dean of the Hofstra University School of Business has said, "Perhaps race will always matter, given the historical circumstances under which we came to this country." But studying this past and understanding how it contributes to present-day dialogues about race and history in America is a critical component of contemporary education. To this end, the Lucent Library of Black History offers a thorough look at the experiences that have shaped the black community and the American people as a whole. Annotated bibliographies provide readers with ideas for further research, while fully documented primary and secondary source quotations enhance the text. Each book in the series explores a different episode of black history; together they provide students with a wealth of information as well as launching points for further study and discussion.

Introduction

The Birth of an American Art Form

Of all the cultural contributions made by African Americans in the United States, jazz rates as one of the greatest. Born in the bars and bordellos of New Orleans during the 1890s, jazz has evolved into a poetic musical form welcomed in fine art centers in cities such as New York, Los Angeles, and Washington, D.C. Once performed by untrained musicians who were unable to read transcribed music, jazz is now taught in prestigious conservatories and colleges.

Jazz has also traveled far beyond the borders of the United States. Even early in its development, American jazz found a warm reception in Europe; today, jazz is embraced all over the world, from Stockholm, Sweden, to Cape Town, South Africa. As an African American art form, jazz is part of a tradition that continues to enrich both the United States and cultures around the world in the present.

Trying to understand how jazz has influenced and intertwined with American culture is not easy. Over time, jazz has seeped into many areas of American life and has taken many forms, including live performances in nightclubs and at high school events, recordings on the radio, and jazz soundtracks on television and in the movies. It is difficult to remember a time when jazz was new and sometimes controversial.

Arguably, jazz has played a central role in the development of American culture.

Often, jazz allowed African Americans an avenue for artistic expression within a larger society that suppressed black creativity. In a variety of ways, jazz has also helped to negotiate race relations in the United States, allowing blacks, whites, and many other races a neutral ground to learn about one another. Even while jazz was initially associated with African Americans, jazz has become part of the social fabric for all Americans. Jazz was born over a hundred years ago, but it remains a living legacy, both in the United States and around the world.

Artistic Expression and Freedom

During the late 1800s, when jazz was first being formed from blues, folk music, and ragtime, many African Americans were treated as second-class citizens in the United States. While slavery had officially ended with the Civil War, many Southern states continued to restrain the freedom of blacks through oppressive laws. Known as Jim Crow laws, these rules robbed African Americans of many basic rights, including the freedom to vote. Many of these laws supported a "separate but equal" philosophy, and enforced racial segregation. Under these laws, blacks and whites attended different schools, ate at different restaurants, and rode on separate train cars. Although separate, the facilities for African Americans were seldom equal.

Performing music became one activity available to blacks who aspired to a life beyond exploitation and Jim Crow restrictions. After the Civil War, a number of black performers traveled in minstrel shows, moving from town to town to perform skits, music, and theater. In New Orleans, Louisiana, after the Civil War, many blacks joined brass marching bands and performed at parties, funerals, and weddings. In a band, African Americans were able to earn money and travel broadly.

The birth of jazz would raise black musicianship to an art form. What made jazz different from the average brass band in New Orleans was improvisation: Instead of following the melody of the song, the jazz player offered creative embellishment; instead of following the predictable pattern as the song was written, the jazz musician followed his or her imagination. Jazz offered a

The mural "The Wall of Respect," in Chicago, Illinois, celebrates the enduring legacy of jazz—a true African American art form.

culturally acceptable way for African Americans to express themselves artistically.

As a form of African American expression, jazz has frequently reflected social and political concerns within the United States. During the 1920s, for instance, jazz formed the musical backdrop in New York City during the time that the Harlem Renaissance— a movement of black poets, writers, and reformers—was taking place. During the 1950s and 1960s, new styles of jazz reflected the struggle within the civil rights movement for black equality. For many black jazz musicians at the time, musical freedom expressed a desire for social and political freedom.

Jazz also provided a neutral meeting ground for blacks, whites, and other races in which they could learn about one another and exchange ideas. Through at least half of the twentieth century

(1900–1950), blacks and whites lived in different neighborhoods and in different sections of most cities. The world of jazz was less concerned with these separations. In the recording studio, on stages and movie screens, and on the dance floor, jazz provided a social setting for black and white cultures to meet and mingle. As jazz brought all races closer together during the twentieth century, jazz became a truly American form of music.

A Living Legacy

Because jazz has such a long history and because jazz is less popular today than more modern music forms such as rock and roll and hip-hop, it is easy to think of jazz as music from the past. Jazz, however, continues to be a living legacy. Jazz as an art form, as a form of black heritage, and as a form of cultural expression remains alive.

The living legacy of jazz is present in the music of the many artists who have long since passed from the scene. While saxophone player Charlie Parker died in 1955, hundreds of his recordings have been preserved for future generations; while the music of trumpeter and singer Louis Armstrong is no longer in style, it remains a rich depository for all who are able to look past the trends of the day. All of this music—available in libraries, on CDs, and as MP3 downloads—continues to live as long as jazz fans continue to listen, enjoy, and learn from these legacies. As a great African American art form, jazz holds within it the triumphs and tragedies of the black experience in the United States. As an expressive form, jazz is the living legacy of a people who overcame adversity to achieve lasting dignity.

This living legacy is also present in the work of many contemporary jazz artists, from the traditionalism of trumpeter Wynton Marsalis to the rap jazz of the Jungle Brothers. Vocalist Cassandra Wilson has combined jazz with blues and even popular songs, recording the Monkees' "Last Train to Clarksville" and Joni Mitchell's "Black Crow." British musician Courtney Pine has pursued a similar path, blending jazz with world, pop, and reggae music to create an eclectic mix on albums like 2004's *Devotion*. The continued growth and expansion of jazz bears witness to the music's ability to express and document the spirit of the black experience in America in the 2000s.

Chapter One

The Roots of Jazz

While the origins of jazz are shrouded in mystery, historians have been able to trace the musical sources that would form the bedrock of jazz to African American culture. The first slaves who arrived in America during the early 1600s brought West African musical traditions to the New World. African Americans played drums, banjo, and flute, sang work songs and spirituals, and practiced call-and-response singing in churches. "Music was in all things," writes jazz historian John Fordham. "There were songs for courtship, for gossip and abuse, songs with rhythms suited to particular tasks, songs of seamanship, worship, and war."[1]

Because songs covered all aspects of the black experience in America, they were about more than entertainment. Folk and gospel songs carried the heritage and traditions of Africa, and they gave witness to the injustice of slavery. Black music documented the story of race in America for blacks, but also served to remind all Americans of the black experience. Black music, even early in American history, would influence all forms of music in the United States, from minstrel songs to gospel music. Black heritage as expressed in music was finally about much more than the black experience: It was a central part of the American experience itself.

This experience along with African American musical heritage blended together in a unique way in the diverse city of New Orleans, Louisiana. Black musical heritage would be influenced by the Creoles of New Orleans, an ethnic group of mixed African, Spanish, and French origin. While blacks and Creoles developed separate cultures in New Orleans, the city included a number of music centers and festivals that allowed both groups to share cultural traditions. From the tradition of African drumming in Congo Square to the marching bands that took part in the annual Mardi Gras celebration, blacks and Creoles combined a variety of musical traditions to create new practices. Together, the musical cultures of blacks and Creoles would be allowed to grow in New Orleans, giving birth to a new American art form.

The ethnic Creoles of New Orleans influenced black musical heritage. New Orleans had several centers that allowed blacks and Creoles to share cultural traditions and music.

New Orleans: The Crescent City

The origins of jazz can be understood against the backdrop of African American, Caribbean, Native American, and European cultures that intermingled in New Orleans during the eighteenth and nineteenth centuries. Jazz historian John F. Szwed says of the city:

> New Orleans was and is America's most exotic city, the bottom of the United States and the top of Latin America, a nexus [center] of cultural development, and in many ways the Athens of the New World. True also that New Orleans was the gathering point (if not the birthplace) of many different musics: jazz historians point to the African songs and dances of Congo Square, the presence of opera, military bands, dance bands, singing street venders, balls and parades.[2]

New Orleans was founded by France on May 7, 1718, and was nicknamed the Crescent City because it is situated in a geographical bend in the Mississippi River. New Orleans was ceded to Spain in 1763, returned to France in 1801, and became a territory of the United States following the Louisiana Purchase during the presidency of Thomas Jefferson in 1803. The early population of the city included French, Americans, Africans, Creoles, Germans, Spanish, and Choctaw and Natchez Indians. Each of these groups brought distinct musical traditions to New Orleans culture.

This broad musical heritage was supported and enriched by New Orleans's geographical location on the Mississippi River, which served as a channel for new immigrants, slaves, and political exiles. Between 1820 and 1860, New Orleans served as the second-largest immigrant port and the largest slave port in the United States. This brought an influx of Germans, Irish, Jews, Creoles, and African Americans into New Orleans, making it one of the most cosmopolitan cities in the United States. Historian Geoffrey C. Ward writes that "New Orleans *was* a sight wholly new, the most cosmopolitan city in the country, perhaps the world."[3] While each ethnic group would contribute to the growth of New Orleans music, African Americans and Creoles would add the essential ingredients in the musical gumbo that would become American jazz.

African American and Creole Culture in New Orleans

While African American and Creole influences would form the bedrock for musical developments in New Orleans throughout the 1800s, these individual groups also developed separate cultures and musical styles.

Following a successful slave uprising in the West Indian country of Haiti in 1804, many of the ousted slave owners immigrated to New Orleans, bringing thousands of African slaves with them. While slavery was firmly established in New Orleans, the city also had a large population of free blacks, equaling one-fifth of the city's inhabitants in 1805. Many of these slaves and free blacks had brought musical traditions from their homeland in West Africa. Within black folk culture, work songs, field hollers, and spirituals were part of everyday African American life. Field hands sang as they worked and this music formed a central part of black worship. "Black music is unity music," says music historian James H. Cone. "It unites the joy and the sorrow, the love and the hate, the hope and the despair of black people."[4]

Many free and enslaved blacks strived to preserve these traditions, gathering on Sunday afternoons in an area known as Congo Square to sell goods, play drums, dance, and perform music. Architect Benjamin Henry Latrobe offered this description of Congo Square:

> The music consisted of two drums and a stringed instrument. An old man sat astride of a cylindrical drum about a foot in diameter, & beat it with incredible quickness with the edge of his hand & fingers. The other drum was an open staved thing held between the knees & beaten in the same manner. They made an incredible noise. The most curious instrument, however, was a stringed instrument, which no doubt was imported from Africa. On the top of the finger board was the rude figure of a man in a sitting posture, & two pegs behind him to which the strings were fastened. The body was a calabash [a type of gourd]. It was played upon by a very little old man, apparently eighty or ninety years old.[5]

While many African musical traditions were suppressed by slave owners throughout the pre–Civil War South, these traditions were preserved and continued to grow in New Orleans.

Another important ethnic group in New Orleans was the Creoles, sometimes referred to as the "Creoles of color." These people were a mixture of the primarily Spanish and French Creoles and the new immigrants from Haiti. Due to their European ancestry, these mixed Creoles were allowed a number of educational opportunities that were denied to African Americans. Creole musicians, for example, were sometimes schooled in classical music, studying at the French Opera House in New Orleans and conservatories in Paris. Because of these opportunities, Creole music was grounded in European classical traditions and frequently diverged from African American music. "Even after the Civil War," writes jazz historian Ted Gioia, "these Creoles of color did not associate with black society; instead, they imitated the ways of the continental European settlers."[6] As African Americans strived to preserve West African culture, Creoles strived to preserve European culture.

The efforts by Creoles and blacks to preserve their unique cultures represented an ongoing effort to define the black experience within America. The growth of both black and Creole cultures also reflected each group's position within American society. Because the daily lives of blacks and Creoles were much different than those of white America, mainstream culture had little to offer either group. This alienation from the mainstream was reinforced by social and legal rules: Blacks and Creoles were purposely separated from white society. Excluded from the mainstream culture as defined by white Americans during the late 1700s and earlier 1800s, blacks and Creoles were forced to create and shape independent cultures.

A Musical Melting Pot

The music of African Americans and Creoles in New Orleans was also influenced by developments throughout the greater United States. Two of the most influential music styles that grew out of folk and popular music during the late 1800s were the blues and ragtime. The blues was imported from the Mississippi Delta and other regions in the South, while ragtime borrowed from European

In the 1800s, New Orleans possessed a cultural mix of African Americans and Creoles, who eventually fused jazz with blues and ragtime.

classical music and grew in cities like St. Louis, Missouri. As musicians traveled to New Orleans by riverboat, train, and overland, they brought these musical influences with them.

The Blues

The blues was a form of folk music born against the backdrop of oppression of African Americans following the end of Reconstruction, the post–Civil War period in which the rebuilding of the American South took place. Following Reconstruction in 1877, the Northern troops that helped in the rebuilding left the South. With them went the resources that had both protected African Americans and helped establish new institutions for blacks, such as schools. As a result, Southern legislatures enacted Jim Crow laws, legislation that limited the rights of African Americans. Blacks, for instance, were required to ride in separate railroad cars and were prevented from voting. The idea that the races should be "separate but equal" was sanctioned by the Supreme Court in 1896 in the landmark decision of *Plessy v. Ferguson*. As a result, blacks within the Southern states would be treated as second-class citizens.

The blues offered blacks an outlet to interpret their cultural experience under Jim Crow in the South. While blacks risked mistreatment for speaking out against Jim Crow, black disapproval could be secretly encoded within a blues song. Jazz historian Gioia writes of early blues music, "The early accounts of slave music are strangely silent about the blues. But should this be any surprise, especially when one considers the use of the idiom [style] to articulate personal statements against oppression and injustice?"[7]

A street scene in Storyville, the famed jazz and blues district of New Orleans in the early 1800s. The first blues songs originated in the Mississippi Delta, not far from New Orleans.

W.C. Handy

W.C. Handy published the first blues song in 1912, and in 1941 he published his memoir, *Father of the Blues: An Autobiography*. Within African American culture, secular forms of music like the blues were sometimes considered sinful. In this selection, Handy recalls the reaction of his minister father to having purchased his first musical instrument.

> When I came into the house, I held the instrument before the eyes of the astonished household. I couldn't speak. I was too full, too overjoyed. Even then, however, I thought I saw something that puzzled me. A shadow seemed to pass over both of my parents. Both of them suddenly lost their voices.
>
> "Look at it shine," I finally said. "It belongs to me—*me*. I saved up the money."
>
> I waited in vain for the expected congratulations. Instead of being pleased, my father was outraged. "Whatever possessed you to bring a sinful thing like that into our home? Take it back where it came from. You hear? Get!"
>
> "A box," he gasped, while my mother stood frozen. "A guitar! One of the devil's playthings. Take it away, I tell you. Get it out of your hands."

W.C. Handy. *Father of the Blues: An Autobiography*. New York: Macmillan, 1941, p. 10.

On the surface the subjects of blues songs were frequently down to earth, covering everyday experiences from work, to hard times, to romantic troubles. These lyrics also incorporated the call-and-response ritual of black spirituals, repeating a statement or question in the first and second lines of a verse, and resolving the statement or answering the question in the third line. A blues song was referred to as twelve-bar blues, representing twelve measures. Blues was performed on guitars, banjos, and flutes. String instruments were particularly useful to blues players, because they allowed the performer to alter the pitch of notes for emotional expression.

Blues historians believe the first blues songs originated in the Mississippi Delta, a stretch of land only a short distance from New Orleans. While historians have been unable to determine definitively when blues began, they have documented the arrival of blues in New Orleans during the 1880s and 1890s. Music historian Ward says of this influx:

> A steady stream of black refugees from the Mississippi Delta was pouring into the city, people for whom even hard labor on the levee promised a better life than any they could hope to have back home, chopping cotton or cutting [sugar]cane. They brought with them as part of their baggage two interrelated forms essential to the development of jazz—the sacred music of the Baptist church and that music's profane twin, the blues.[8]

The arrival of refugees from the Mississippi Delta would add one more flavor to the musical stew of New Orleans—ragtime.

Ragtime

As with the blues, ragtime was an important development in the growth of African American music. As a popular style, ragtime preceded jazz in the 1870s and 1880s and then mirrored the early development of jazz between the 1890s and 1910s. The name ragtime derived from common musical terms like rag and ragging and featured syncopated, or ragged, rhythm. While standard rhythms flow smoothly, syncopation emphasizes unequal, or irregular, rhythm, which provides an element of surprise in ragtime. Jazz historian Barry Ulanov describes ragtime technique as follows:

> What ragtime contributed to jazz in its brisk forays up and down the piano keyboard . . . was a respect for a complete command of instrumental technique and an understanding of the place a composer could have in music that which was largely improvised. These valuable contributions and a repertory of rags that could sustain almost any kind of improvisational mayhem give ragtime an important place in the early history of jazz.[9]

Ragtime existed as both vocal and instrumental music and between the late 1890s and 1918 became the most popular form of music in America.

Ragtime instrumentals were widely distributed by way of sheet music, the printed form of music notation, and piano rolls, rolls of paper that stored the music that operated self-playing pianos.

The cover of the sheet music for Scott Joplin's song "The Entertainer." Joplin expanded the horizons of piano-based ragtime.

Sheet music and piano rolls allowed anyone with access to an instrument to perform the popular ragtime songs of the day, and the piano was the perfect instrument for the syncopated rhythms of ragtime. Reflecting the popularity of ragtime, piano sales sky-rocketed, reaching a high in 1909 of about 350,000 pianos sold. Newly written instrumentals, such as Scott Joplin's "The Enter-tainer" and "Maple Leaf Rag," also expanded the artistic quality of piano-based ragtime. "Ragtime reached its highest musical de-velopment," notes music historian John Edward Hasse, "as an in-strumental music."[10]

Despite the talent and quality of the work of Joplin and others, most jazz historians do not consider ragtime to be jazz. While the jagged ragtime rhythms would add an essential element to the musical makeup of jazz, ragtime usually followed more rigid guidelines than jazz. These guidelines, historians have noted, were related to the European classical tradition. "Ragtime is America's equivalent to classical music rather than an actual jazz style,"[11] writes jazz journalist Scott Yanow. As with classical music, rag-time performers played from sheet music, leaving less room for personal interpretation, or improvising.

Whereas musicians from the Mississippi Delta had brought the blues to New Orleans, ragtime performers introduced their song style in the form of sheet music, piano rolls, and in person by way of cities like St. Louis. Soon, black and Creole musicians in New Orleans adapted ragtime into their live performances and ragtime, like the blues, became part of the foundation of the New Orleans vibrant musical culture.

Blacks and Creoles in New Orleans During the 1890s

The musical cultures of blacks and Creoles were influenced by ragtime and the blues, but each group began to develop separate musical cultures in New Orleans during the late 1800s. Many Creole musicians were able to read music and because of the lightness of their skin, they were sometimes allowed to join white musical groups. At the time, African Americans could seldom read music and were forced to form their own separate bands. When marching bands became very popular after the Civil War

James P. Johnson

———————◼———————

James P. Johnson was a pianist and important ragtime composer during the early 1900s. In this selection, Johnson recalls his development as a composer during the 1910s.

I had started to compose my first rag about this time (1914), but nothing was done with it, and I threw it away. I also wrote and threw away a number of songs, although some people liked them.

. . .

Then I met Will Farrell, a Negro song writer, and he showed me how to set my pieces down in writing. He also wrote lyrics for them. With him, I set down my first composition to be published, "Mamma's and Pappa's Blues." . . .

With Farrell, I also wrote "Stop It, Joe!" at the time. I sold it, along with "Mamma's and Pappa's Blues" for twenty-five dollars apiece to get enough money for a deposit on a grand piano.

John Edward Hasse, ed. *Ragtime: Its History, Composers, and Music.* New York: Schirmer, 1985, pp. 175–176.

in New Orleans, both blacks and Creoles formed brass bands. Although they played similar styles of music and performed at similar venues, such as funeral processions, the two groups never united in the same bands.

This separation was evident in all aspects of black and Creole culture throughout the 1870s and 1880s. Many Creoles identified with European ancestry, continued to speak French, and practiced Catholicism; while most blacks identified with African American heritage, spoke English, and practiced Protestant Christianity or voodoo, a religion based on a mixture of traditional African beliefs and Catholicism. In the 1890s, however, Jim Crow laws would change the relationship between Creoles and blacks in New Orleans. In 1894 Louisiana Legislative Code No. 111 "specified that anyone with any black ancestry, however remote, would be considered black."[12] Now, from a legal standpoint, there was no difference between the Creoles and blacks.

The legislative code had less immediate impact on African Americans than Creoles, as blacks already had few rights in the post-Reconstruction South. The legislation, however, would have a tremendous economic impact on the Creole community. Jazz historian Leroy Ostransky notes, "Whites could no longer do business with them [Creoles] nor patronize their shops. The boycott, although not formally organized, was nonetheless strong and pervasive."[13]

Many Creole artists and musicians were particularly hard hit: Because of the new status designation that discounted the Creoles' white heritage, finding jobs in white musical groups became difficult. As Creole musicians searched for new places to perform, they found themselves in competition with and, over time, in cooperation with black musicians. This tension and then collaboration would bring many styles of New Orleans music together.

Jazz Is Born

The combination and competition of black and Creole musicians during the 1890s led to the mingling of blues, ragtime, and marching band music in dance halls, restaurants, and nightclubs throughout New Orleans. "Suddenly these polished Creole ensembles were forced to compete for work against the less schooled, more boisterous black bands that were pursuing a 'hotter' style," writes jazz historian Gioia, "one that would serve as the foundation for jazz."[14]

While nobody can say with certainty when jazz first emerged in New Orleans, jazz journalists and historians have been willing to offer educated guesses. The editors of the *All Music Guide to Jazz* have speculated that although the origins of jazz may remain unknown, marching bands may have been the first to perform the new music:

> One of the major questions that will go forever unanswered is "How did jazz start?" The first jazz recording was in 1917, but the music existed in at least primitive forms for 20 years before that. Influenced by classical music, marches, spirituals, work songs, ragtime, blues, and the popular music of the period, jazz was already a distinctive form of music by the time it was first documented.

Buddy Bolden

Buddy Bolden was born in 1877, and many jazz historians believe he was the first genius of jazz. In the following selection, the clarinetist George Baquet remembers seeing Bolden play in Odd Fellows Hall in New Orleans:

> Nobody took their hats off. It was plenty rough. You paid fifteen cents and walked in. The band, six of them, was sitting on a low stand. They had their hats on and were resting, pretty sleepy. All of a sudden, Buddy stomps, knocks on the floor with his trumpet to give the beat and they all sit up straight. They played "Make Me a Pallet." Everybody rose and yelled out, "Oh, Mr. Bolden, play it for us, Buddy play it!" I'd never heard anything like it before. I'd played "legitimate" stuff. But this, it was something that pulled me in. They got me up on the stand and I played with them. After that I didn't play legitimate so much.

Quoted in Geoffrey C. Ward and Ken Burns, *Jazz: A History of America's Music*. New York: Knopf, 2000, p. 22.

This rare circa 1900 photograph shows the Buddy Bolden Band. Bolden, standing second from left, is considered by many to be the father of jazz.

The chances are that the earliest jazz was played by un-schooled musicians in New Orleans marching bands. Music was a major part of life in New Orleans from at least the 1890s with brass bands hired to play at parades, funerals, parties and dances. It stands to reason that the musicians (who often did not read music) did not simply play the melodies continuously but came up with variations to keep the performances interesting.[15]

It has also been speculated that a New Orleans African American cornet player named Buddy Bolden was the father of jazz. Bolden formed a band during the mid-1890s, one that offered a variation on the brass bands of the era and included cornet, two clarinets, guitar, bass, valve trombone, and drums. Although no known recording of Bolden and his band has survived, he became known in New Orleans for songs like "Buddy Bolden's Blues."

Whether considering an anonymous brass band or Bolden's ensemble, what made the new music jazz instead of ragtime or blues was the variation on the melody. While a clarinetist in a jazz band played the melody of "Buddy Bolden's Stomp," the cornet player added flourishes that deviated from that melody. In early jazz, several players might improvise all at once, or in another variation, the trombone and tuba might follow one another, working like the call and response of a black spiritual. "Essentially jazz is music that puts an emphasis on improvisation and always has the feeling of the blues,"[16] notes jazz journalist Yanow. The reputation of jazz players would be built on the creative ability of improvising with feeling.

Soon, the new art of improvising would grow into new styles of jazz in New Orleans, and the musicians who played the new music would export jazz to cities all over the United States and around the world.

Chapter Two

Early Jazz from New Orleans to Chicago (1900–1930)

After the birth of jazz in New Orleans in the mid-1890s, this new music form evolved quickly. A variety of styles—from New Orleans jazz, to Dixieland, to classic jazz—would succeed and often overlap one another between 1900 and 1930. The ensemble style of the 1910s, featuring musicians in bands who played simultaneously with one another, would give way to the solo style during the 1920s, featuring the improvising skills of individuals. The focus on the jazz solo would give rise to new stars within jazz, including a young Louis Armstrong. Like the expansion of styles, jazz would expand beyond the borders of New Orleans during this period. While New Orleans remained the jazz capital during the 1910s, Chicago would fill that role during the 1920s. During what novelist F. Scott Fitzgerald would call the Jazz Age, the new music reached all Americans.

These changes and overlapping styles would take place against a backdrop of rapidly evolving black culture. A great deal of the black experience had been forged in the American South, where slavery and second-class citizenship had been considered the norm. During this era, many blacks left the South in hopes of finding better economic and social opportunities in Northeastern cities. While migrating would have a significant impact on black culture, it also served to spread Southern black culture throughout the United States. In the same way that slaves had brought music and customs from Africa to America, Southern blacks would bring the music and customs of New Orleans, Atlanta, and other locales to New York, Chicago, and Philadelphia. In a short time jazz, which was little more than a regional style during its infancy, would become a national music form embraced by whites and blacks alike.

New Orleans Jazz: 1900–1917

In 1906 a number of jazz performers took center stage in New Orleans. Cornet players Freddie Keppard and King Oliver, trombonist Kid Ory, pianist Jelly Roll Morton, and clarinetists Sidney Bechet and Johnny Dodds were among the most influential jazz musicians between 1906 and 1917. Because these players lived in New Orleans during at least part of this time period, the music they performed became known as New Orleans jazz. "Arguably the happiest of all forms of music is New Orleans jazz and its later descendant Dixieland,"[17] notes jazz journalist Scott Yanow.

A hallmark of New Orleans jazz was ensemble-style playing. In ensemble-style jazz, each player has an assigned role, allowing a dynamic interplay between a large group of musicians. Unlike later jazz, solos by individual players in ensemble-style jazz are rare. Jazz teacher Mark C. Gridley explains ensemble-style jazz:

> These early bands featured choruses in which every player was creating phrases which complemented every other player's phrases. For many listeners, the greatest appeal of early jazz is the activity of several horn lines sounding at the same time without clashing. Musicians managed to stay out of each other's way partly because they tended to fulfill set musical roles similar to those established for their instruments in brass bands. The trumpet often played the melody. The clarinet played busy figures with many notes. The clari-

net part decorated the melody played by the trumpet. The trombone would play simpler figures. . . . The skills of the improviser who was required to blend with the collectivity improvised phrases of other players differed from the skills of the improviser who was required to solo dramatically.[18]

Other instruments—the guitar, piano, drums, bass, and banjo—kept rhythm and time.

Kid Ory, an originator of New Orleans jazz, continued to play trombone for decades.

Two early bandleaders displayed the full-flowering of New Orleans jazz: Keppard and Ory. Keppard was the heir to Bolden's crown in 1906, and he joined Frankie Dusen's Eagle Band between 1907 and 1911. Beginning in 1912, Keppard co-led the Original Creole Orchestra. In 1916 Keppard was offered an opportunity to record at Victor Records, but he declined. "One legend says that Keppard didn't want his style copied," notes jazz historian Marshall W. Stearns, "another legend insists that the record executives decided that Keppard played too 'hot and dirty' for the family trade."[19] Whatever the reason, the decision not to record Keppard proved significant to early jazz history: The first jazz musicians to record would be white, not black.

Trombonist Ory came to prominence in 1912 and is referred to by jazz writer Yanow as "one of the great New Orleans pioneers."[20] He recruited many of the most talented musicians in New Orleans, including clarinetist Dodds and trumpeter Armstrong. Ory also influenced the development of what was referred to as cutting contests in New Orleans. To advertise performances, jazz bands would ride around the city in a horse-drawn wagon, performing songs to entice patrons. When one band met another, a cutting contest ensued. Both bands would take turns performing, trying to cut, or outperform, the other band, while bystanders determined the winner. Cutting contests revealed the sometimes competitive nature of early jazz in New Orleans: There was a limited number of paying customers, and bands worked hard to attract them.

While jazz would continue to flourish throughout the 1910s in New Orleans, the city's reputation as the center of the jazz world began to shift after 1917. Commentators have frequently noted that this change coincided with the closing of Storyville, New Orleans's red light district that employed many of the city's musicians. The federal government closed Storyville during World War I against strong objections from New Orleans government officials, citing the area as a negative influence on American soldiers. Historically, however, the closing of Storyville may have had less impact on jazz than other changes that were taking place within the city. A number of New Orleans musicians had gone on the road in the late 1910s, traveling and performing throughout the United States. Ory, for instance, had traveled as far as Los

Twelve-year-old Louis Armstrong, center of second row from top, was a member of the Waif's Home Colored Brass Band.

Angeles. On the road, jazz musicians discovered opportunities that were not available in New Orleans. Still, the closing of Storyville served as a symbolic end for the early jazz era. "By 1917," writes jazz historian Stearns, "Storyville was closed, New Orleans was sunk in a business depression, and jazzmen were looking north for employment."[21]

First Jazz Recordings

One of the opportunities musicians found in big cities from New York to Los Angeles was the chance to make records in recording studios. Between the birth of jazz in the mid-1890s and the time before jazz began to expand in 1916, no jazz was ever recorded, meaning that the music of the first twenty years of jazz's existence had not been officially preserved. Jazz fans would later interview many early jazz musicians, however, to help establish early practices. It has been speculated that jazz, as a new kind of music, was under the radar for many talent scouts and recording companies. Another obstacle was the absence of recording facilities in New Orleans compared to what was available in cities like New York and Chicago. "Recording activity in New Orleans was sparse at first, so a few key musicians in that city never recorded at all,"[22] writes jazz historian and author John F. Szwed in *Jazz 101*. Because of a lack of early recordings, there is no documentation of how early jazz sounded.

Critics have even questioned how well the first jazz recording, by the Original Dixieland Jazz Band, represented the sounds of early jazz. The 1917 recording of "Livery Stable Blues" for Columbia Records in New York City created, and continues to create, controversy. This controversy revolved around a simple fact: The first band to record jazz, a music born out of African American

The Original Dixieland Jazz Band's first jazz recordings caused, and continue to cause, much controversy because they were an all-white group that recorded music born of the African American culture.

culture, was white. "Having declared them [the Original Dixie-land Jazz Band] white imitators performing an inferior version of the real thing," notes Szwed, "the writers of jazz history were unhappy to see them be the first to record."[23]

It took five more years before the first recordings by African American jazz musicians were produced. A series of significant recordings by New Orleans transplants soon followed in the early 1920s. While working in Los Angeles in 1921 and 1922, Ory and his band recorded "Ory's Creole Trombone" and "Society's Blues." Unfortunately, these recordings were for a small record label and received little distribution. Oliver followed in 1923, recording his signature composition "Dippermouth Blues." Among others who recorded during this period, both pianist Morton and trumpeter Armstrong would make noteworthy recordings in Chicago.

Recordings would accomplish more than simply document the early performances of jazz musicians. In the early 1920s, re-cordings also allowed the new music to reach a national audience, playing a pivotal role in the nationalization of jazz. In 1921, 100 million records were produced in the United States, 75 percent more than had been made in 1914. Jazz, while not the dominant style of music in 1921, nonetheless represented an expanding and increasingly popular musical form. Jazz writer Kurt Gartner explains the importance of developing technology to jazz:

> Technology facilitated the growing prominence of jazz. Mechanical and electronic reproductions of performances became available nationally through player piano scrolls, published sheet music, radio broadcasts, and wax cylinder (later, phonograph) recordings. In fact, the inception and development of jazz music closely parallels the chronology of the development of audio recordings and mass repro-duction techniques. Of course, access to early recordings provides ample opportunities for present-day research and enjoyment. Access to these recordings in the 1920s allowed musicians to study and influence each other's performances with greatly reduced barriers of time, distance, and stigmas of racial prejudice.[24]

Recordings allowed the influence of jazz to spread beyond a band's home base. While jazz recordings by black musicians would influence many white musicians, these recordings also reached the homes of many white and nonwhite listeners, offering an undiluted artifact of African American culture. By the early 1920s, jazz songs and instrumentals could be recorded in a studio, pressed into thousands of shellac discs, distributed by trains and trucks, and placed in stores across the nation in a short span of time.

Exodus to Chicago

One irony of the early jazz age was that many recordings that would introduce New Orleans style jazz to a broader world were made in Chicago. Jazz teacher Gridley notes, "What is usually referred to as New Orleans style is not the music that was played between 1900 and 1920 in New Orleans—we have never heard that music because it was not recorded—but rather the music recorded by New Orleans musicians in Chicago during the 1920s."[25]

Chicago acted as a magnet for New Orleans musicians, offering more opportunities and more money. In 1919 following the historic period known as Prohibition, which restricted the consumption and sale of alcohol in the United States, Chicago earned a reputation as a city teeming with nightclubs, illegal whisky, and gangsters. For many musicians, relocating to Chicago opened a new world of work-related opportunities in cabarets, roadhouses, and dance halls.

While many musicians moved to Chicago for its economic advantages, they formed part of a larger movement known as the Great Migration. This migration was spurred when World War I began, preventing Europeans from immigrating and working in American industry and therefore opening up opportunities for blacks. Between 1914 and 1919, over three hundred thousand African Americans left the South, searching for work and for racial equality in the North. Another 1 million blacks would migrate north during the 1920s. This migration included all segments of African American society, from musicians, to doctors, to laborers.

Musicians moved for many of the same reasons as other Southern blacks: Work in the South was scarce. Even in New Orleans's famed Storyville prior to 1917 there was a limited number of venues where jazz musicians could play. This forced many musicians

African American Migration, 1914–1919

Between 1914 and 1919, African Americans began moving north in large numbers. In the publication *The New Negro*, author Alain Locke explains the reasons blacks were leaving the South:

> The tide of Negro migration, northward and cityward, is not to be fully explained as a blind flood started by the demands of war industry coupled with the shutting off of foreign immigration, or by the pressure of poor crops coupled with increased social terrorism in certain sections of the South and Southwest. Neither labor demand, the boll weevil, nor the Ku Klux Klan is a basic factor, however contributory any or all of them may have been. The wash and rush of this human tide on the beach line of the northern city centers is to be explained primarily in terms of a new vision of opportunity, of social and economic freedom, of a spirit to seize, even in the face of an extortionate and heavy toll, a chance for the improvement of conditions. With each successive wave of it, the movement toward the larger and the more democratic chance—in the Negro's case a deliberate flight not only from countryside to city, but from medieval America to modern.

Quoted in Geoffrey C. Ward, *Jazz: A History of America's Music*. New York: Knopf, 2000, p. 85.

to maintain day jobs while playing music at night in order to earn a living. Jazz historian Ted Gioia writes:

> Musicians moved north for the same reasons that motivated other groups: the search for a better life, for greater opportunities to work, to support a family, to enjoy a modicum [moderate amount] of personal freedom—options that were much harder for an African American to pursue in the segregated South.[26]

Although Chicago offered black musicians opportunities unavailable in New Orleans, they were still relegated to what was referred to as the "black belt" in the city and were generally paid less than white musicians. Nonetheless, the looser racial code of Chicago occasionally allowed black and white musicians to record and perform together. This permitted black and white musicians to share with and influence one another.

From New Orleans Style to Classic Jazz

In Chicago, Morton, Oliver, and Armstrong would quickly transform New Orleans jazz into something new and exciting. While classic jazz retained many elements of the New Orleans style of jazz, the two styles parted in a fundamental way: Whereas New Orleans jazz had featured ensemble-style performances, classic jazz would highlight the soloist. Morton, Oliver, and Armstrong, as jazz musicians, as bandleaders, as composers, and as singers, would revolutionize jazz between 1923 and 1928.

Jelly Roll Morton

Pianist Morton began his career in New Orleans, learning his trade in the bordellos of Storyville. By 1908, however, he had left New Orleans to travel throughout the United States. Morton relocated to Chicago in 1923, and would begin one of the most prolific periods of his life as a jazz player. He continuously made records and piano rolls between 1923 and 1926, perhaps as many as one hundred, and formed his best-known group, the Red Hot Peppers. "This band," historian Gioia says of the Red Hot Peppers, "achieved a level of collective artistry that few New Orleans groups ever matched, and none surpassed."[27]

Morton's greatest gift to early jazz was his talent as a composer. "His [Morton's] piano pieces were thoroughly orchestral, virtual arrangements with the various instruments' parts clearly audible in the playing, just waiting to be transferred to a band,"[28] writes Szwed in his book *Jazz 101*. He created intricate arrangements out of sources as varied as popular dance songs and Caribbean folk tunes. Because of this intricacy, Morton demanded that the musicians that he worked with follow his instructions exactly. In one story about Morton's methods in the studio, a trombonist refused to perform a melody as it had been written for a recording session. The following day Morton placed a pistol on top of the piano, encouraging the trombonist to play the composition as it had been written.

Jelly Roll Morton and his Red Hot Peppers, with Morton at piano and Kid Ory on trombone, in Chicago in 1926. According to one jazz historian the band "achieved a level of collective artistry that few New Orleans groups ever matched, and none surpassed."

In retrospect, a number of critics have perhaps overlooked Morton's abilities because of his tendency to overstate his importance in the creation of jazz. Morton served as a key figure in the evolution of the piano from ragtime to jazz, and his compositional work would remain influential to later bandleaders like Duke Ellington and Charles Mingus. "Although Morton did not invent jazz," notes historian Gioia, "he was perhaps the first to think about it in abstract terms, and articulate . . . a coherent theoretical approach to its creation."[29] Despite his innovations, however, Morton's carefully planned style of jazz would soon lose favor to a freer form of jazz invented by other New Orleans alumni.

King Oliver

Following in the footsteps of Ory, cornet player Oliver became the central jazz performer in New Orleans during the 1910s. Like Ory, Oliver was in the habit of hiring the most talented players for his band. "There is no question," states jazz writer Leroy Ostransky, "that Oliver and the musicians he gathered about him have to be reckoned among the historically most significant figures in early jazz."[30] By 1922 Oliver had relocated to Chicago and the following year, completed his first recordings.

Oliver's arrival in Chicago helped establish the city as the center of jazz for the next five years. He formed the Creole Jazz Band and performed at Lincoln Gardens, drawing large crowds that included other musicians. "Had the Oliver band simply continued to play its regular sessions at the Lincoln Gardens," notes jazz historian Alyn Shipton, "it is unlikely that it would have had the considerable impact on the development of jazz that it did."[31] In April 1923 Oliver and his band entered the studio to record several instrumentals, including his signature piece, "Dippermouth Blues." These recordings were very influential to other jazz musicians of the era.

Before these recordings were made, Oliver made a decision that would change the face of jazz in the mid-1920s: In early 1923 he invited cornet player Armstrong to Chicago to become a member of his band. Since both Oliver and Armstrong played the cornet, this was an unusual—perhaps unheard-of—move, as no jazz band had two cornet players. It also posed a risk to Oliver. By allowing a second cornet player into the band, there was always the possibility that his protégé would outshine him. With Armstrong in his band, Oliver's music provided a bridge between more traditional New Orleans jazz and the newer innovations that would emerge in the mid-1920s.

Louis Armstrong

Of all of the figures to perform classic jazz, Armstrong remains the most influential. "Louis Armstrong," notes jazz writer Szwed, "is arguably the most important musician that the United States has ever produced."[32] First as a member of Oliver's band and then on his own, Armstrong served as the central figure in pushing jazz

Chicago Nightclubs

Despite the importance of recordings to the spread of jazz during the mid-1920s, most musicians made their living performing nightly in cabarets and roadhouses. In the following account, early-jazz historian Frederick Ramsey Jr. sketches the atmosphere of a typical night at Lincoln Gardens where King Oliver and Louis Armstrong performed in 1923:

> There were no waltzes played at the Lincoln Gardens, the customers liked the Bunny-hug, the Charleston, the Black Bottom. . . . Joe [King Oliver] tooted a few notes down low to the orchestra, stomped his feet to give the beat, turned around, and they were off on a new piece. . . . Lil Hardin bit hard on her four beats to a measure [piano], while the deep beat of Bill Johnson's string bass and the clearly defined foundation of Baby Dodds' drum and high-toned, biting cymbal filled out the "bounce" and kept the others swinging forward. This motion led to a climax, a point beyond which the breathless pace of the music seemed doomed to fall, unless something would intervene. Then Joe and Louis [Armstrong] stepped out, and one of their "breaks" came rolling out of the two short horns, fiercely and flawlessly.

Quoted in Lee Ostransky, *Jazz City: The Impact of Our Cities on the Development of Jazz.* Englewood Cliffs, NJ: Prentice-Hall, 1978, p. 108.

King Oliver's Creole Jazz Band included Louis Armstrong, standing in middle, on trumpet. The highlight of their Chicago nightclub shows were King Oliver and Armstrong's trumpet jams on stage.

Between 1925 and 1928 Louis Armstrong's Hot Fives Band, including (from right to left) his wife, Lil Hardin, Kid Ory, Johnny Dodds, and Johnny St. Cyr (next to Armstrong, seated), made a series of landmark recordings that are considered jazz masterpieces today.

into a new direction during the mid-1920s in Chicago. It is also believed that Armstrong switched from the cornet to the trumpet during the mid-1920s, believing that the trumpet blended better with other jazz instruments.

After leaving Oliver's band, Armstrong embarked on a series of legendary recordings. These sessions, known as the *Hot Fives* and *Hot Sevens*, were recorded by Armstrong and studio bands beginning on November 12, 1925. Over the next three years, Armstrong recorded dozens of tracks for Okeh Records, an independent record label that would be bought by Columbia in 1926. "Surely no other body of work in the jazz idiom has been so loved and admired as the results of these celebrated sessions,"[33] writes jazz historian Gioia. To make these recordings, Armstrong gathered other New Orleans friends in the studio, including his wife, pianist Lil Hardin Armstrong. In addition to these sessions, Armstrong experimented with different instrumental settings, joining with pianist Earl Hines for another important recording session in 1928.

Armstrong also became well known as a vocalist. While he was not the first person to sing scat—nonsense syllables set to music—he was one of the first performers to make a recording that included scat singing. Armstrong would later claim that he first started scatting when he dropped the lyric sheet to "Heebie Jeebies" during a recording session and was forced to ad-lib. He recalled that day, saying:

> The day we recorded "Heebie Jeebies," I dropped the paper with the lyrics—right in the middle of the tune. . . . And I did not want to stop and spoil the record which was moving along so wonderfully. . . . So when I dropped the paper, I immediately turned back into the horn [recording horn] and started to Scatting. . . . Just as nothing had happened. . . . When I finished the record I just knew the recording people would throw it out. . . . And to my surprise they all came running out of the controlling booth and said—"Leave That In."[34]

While Armstrong's style of scat singing undoubtedly influenced many other singers, it also had a direct impact on record sales. "'Heebie Jeebies' became his first substantial hit," commented jazz historian Shipton on Armstrong, "selling some tens of thousands [of copies]."[35] Jazz trumpeter Wynton Marsalis would recall Armstrong's legacy:

> What Louis Armstrong brought to the world when he started giving notice through his horn in the 1920s had never existed before. This man stood up there and *improvised* music that made perfect sense, that expressed intellect and emotion *in action*. He brought new angles of melody and rhythm into the world. Louis Armstrong was a great artist, one of the greatest of all time, and, as Albert Murray points out in his classic, *Stomping the Blues*, Louis Armstrong's work made him a hero. . . . Jazz is a serious business and it is also the noble joy that Louis Armstrong embodied and projected with his horn. He raised the level of individual confidence. The same recognition of deep human values that you hear in Beethoven, you hear in Louis Armstrong.[36]

Women Blues Singers

———————————◼———————————

Along with the expansion of jazz, the blues reached a popular audience beginning in 1920 with the release of Mamie Smith's "Crazy Blues." Women blues singers were frequently backed by jazz musicians, and many early recordings were made in Chicago. In the following passage, black music historian James Haskins notes the rising popularity of blues singer Ma Rainey during the 1920s, along with the challenges that many black performers faced when traveling:

> That year [1923], she . . . managed to get a recording contract with Paramount Record Company and went to Chicago to make her first recordings. With those recordings, Ma Rainey moved from popular southern singer to a singer of nationwide recognition. "Bad Luck Blues," "Moonshine Blues," and other songs were a balm to the ears of the newly arrived blacks in northern cities. As last they could buy records that featured real down-home music. . . . Ma Rainey's records also sold well in the South, of course. Paramount booked her on the Theater Owners Booking Association (T.O.B.A.) circuit, the major black entertainment circuit, and she performed throughout the South and the Midwest. She was almost constantly on the road, and for a black entertainer in those days— especially one who was a hard-living forty years old—that was not easy. She had to travel on segregated trains and was denied service in segregated dining cars and in hotels and restaurants in the towns where she played.

James Haskins. *Black Music in America*. New York: Thomas Y. Crowell, pp. 74–75.

Ma Rainey was an early blues singer who had to travel by segregated trains and was denied service in segregated dining cars, hotels, and restaurants in the towns she played.

As these recordings reached other musicians, Armstrong's influence would bring one era to a close while it opened another. The ensemble-style jazz born in New Orleans had been transformed into a soloist's art in Chicago. Furthermore, Armstrong's journey from New Orleans to Chicago gave notice that jazz was no longer regional music: Jazz, during the 1920s, had reached all Americans. In this sense, Armstrong became jazz's foremost ambassador, introducing audiences and record buyers to a new form of music. "One of jazz's first true virtuosos," writes jazz journalist Yanow, "his influence over his contemporaries was so powerful that nearly every trumpeter to record between 1927 and 1940 sounded to an extent like one of his followers!"[37] By championing the solo style, Armstrong would help set the stage for new developments in jazz, leading to larger ensembles and more complex arrangements.

Chapter Three

Harlem and the Big Band Era (1925–1946)

While Chicago had reigned as the capital of the jazz world during the mid-1920s, jazz had also established itself in other American cities, including New York, Los Angeles, and Kansas City, Missouri. During the late 1920s, many of the top Chicago performers relocated to Harlem, a section of New York City, adding jazz to the emerging renaissance in black culture. In Harlem jazz pianists began to expand on the tradition of ragtime by creating new styles, while jazz bands were growing larger and developing new ways of arranging popular music. Harlem continued to be an important center for jazz during the 1930s, but big bands would nationalize jazz in the mid-1930s, making big band jazz, also known as swing, the most popular music in America.

The nationalization of jazz also represented the nationalization of African American culture. From the black renaissance in Harlem to nightclubs of Kansas City, blacks came to the forefront in American arts as painters, novelists, poets, and musicians. These artists portrayed both the joy of new possibilities for black America and the racial barriers that served as roadblocks to black progress. While black America had many of the same aspirations as all of America, educational and economic opportunities often remained limited to blacks. As black musicians continued to excel within jazz as innovators, white musicians who sometimes played the same music often reached larger audiences and earned more money.

Therefore, the expansion of jazz to a national audience was filled with both hope and hardship for black Americans. Part of that hope was that jazz might be seen as a universal language that everyone, regardless of color, could sing along with, dance to, and celebrate. During this era, jazz became more than a form of music enriched and inspired by the African American experience. It also became America's music, offering a bridge between white and black cultures.

Jazz and the Harlem Renaissance

When black musicians arrived in Harlem from Chicago in the late 1920s, they found themselves in the midst of a cultural awakening that was referred to as the Harlem Renaissance. Consisting of poets, playwrights, social thinkers, and novelists, the renaissance opened a new world of creativity for blacks in America. While many African Americans had struggled to physically survive and maintain a culture in the South, within Harlem blacks were encouraged to build a new society fueled by imagination and a like-minded community. Historian Lee Ostransky notes of the movement:

> Black cultural leaders saw the Harlem Renaissance as the first creative outburst of blacks who had been brought together from all parts of the world to the private and special world of Harlem. The magic of Harlem, the argument went, had brought all these forces together, and now, in the 1920s, the creativity was about to be released, and the white world would come to recognize that which they had tried to contain and suffocate.[38]

Jazz established itself in Harlem as it had in Chicago, with musicians performing in nightclubs like the 101 Ranch, the Band Box, and the Yeah Man. Although Harlem had a growing middle class, jazz musicians frequently lived and performed in the

The Harlem Renaissance

Langston Hughes was a leading literary voice in the Harlem Renaissance. In the following passage, he emphasizes the emergence of artistic Harlem blacks and the interdependence they still had on white America. As Hughes explains, blacks had to rely on whites to publish the manuscripts and produce the music that came from talented black Americans during the renaissance. Race, even within the confines of Harlem, was contentious.

> I soon learned that it was seemingly impossible for black Harlem to live without white downtown. My youthful illusion that Harlem was a world unto itself did not last very long. It was not even an area unto itself. The famous night clubs were owned by whites, as were the theatres. Almost all of the stores were owned by whites. . . . The books of Harlem writers all had to be published downtown, if they were to be published at all. . . . Negroes could not even play their own numbers with their *own* people. Almost all the policemen in Harlem were white. Negroes couldn't even get graft [work] from *themselves* for themselves by themselves.

Quoted in Lee Ostransky, *Jazz City: The Impact of Our Cities on the Development of Jazz.* Englewood Cliffs, NJ: Prentice-Hall, 1978, pp. 188–189.

Langston Hughes was a leading voice of the Harlem Renaissance, and wrote that despite blacks' success in Harlem, they were still dependent on whites.

poorer parts of town. Jazz historian Ted Gioia writes, "Jazz was very much a part of this second [poorer] Harlem, more at home here than in the 'other' Harlem of high culture and higher aspirations."[39] The jazz musicians, like many other residents of Harlem, struggled to pay the bills. One way struggling jazz musicians could raise money was to hold what was known as a rent party. These lively parties featured a jazz band and charged admission. The collected admission would then be used to pay the rent of an apartment or loft.

While both the arts and jazz scenes appeared complementary in retrospect, they formed two separate worlds within Harlem during the late 1920s and 1930s. "Developments in Harlem," writes early jazz historian Marshall W. Stearns, "were complicated."[40] A number of middle-class blacks in Harlem who had embraced the renaissance of black culture rejected jazz for several reasons. Jazz reminded some blacks who had migrated north of life in the South. There was a great psychological difference between the rough-and-tumble rent parties in the poorer sections of Harlem and the gatherings of middle-class literary circles. Jazz was also considered primitive to many within the Harlem movement, a reminder of church music, the blues, and folk songs. Jazz historian John Leland notes the inner conflict within the Harlem community:

> In many conservative African-American households, blues and jazz were the sounds of sin; spirituals filled the air (though truly proper households banned these, too, as uncultured). . . . As the jazz saxophonist Benny Carter said, "We sensed that the black cultural as well as moral leaders looked down on our music as undignified."[41]

Because of these differences, jazz, for the most part, developed outside of the Harlem Renaissance.

Pianos and Stride

During the late 1920s and early 1930s, in a transition between the classic jazz of Chicago and the big bands, jazz pianists helped establish a new culture and style of playing within Harlem. "It's not going too far," writes historian Gioia, "to suggest that the piano was to Harlem what brass bands had been to New Orleans."[42]

Pianist and composer James P. Johnson plays stride style on the piano at a New York studio jam session. In Harlem the piano replaced the brass band as as the driving force of jazz.

Pianist and composer James P. Johnson later recalled why the piano was central to New York jazz:

> The other sections of the country never developed the piano as far as the New York boys did. Only lately have they caught up. The reason the New York boys became such high class musicians was because the New York piano was developed by the European method, system and style. The people in New York were used to hearing good piano played in concerts and cafes. The ragtime player had to live up to that standard. They had to get orchestral effects, sound harmonies, chords, and all the techniques of European concert pianists who were playing their music all over the city.[43]

These new styles also reflected and built on the ragtime tradition, drawing from the work of Johnson, Scott Joplin, and Earl Hines.

The new style of piano music would be called stride. Stride featured a steady rhythm with the pianist's left hand, alternating between bass notes and mid-range chords. With the steady stride of the left hand creating rhythmic support, the right hand was free to wander, improvising a rich flow of melody. Each pianist developed this basic stride blueprint in a different way, creating an individual style highlighted by harmony, dexterity, and speed.

Leading practitioners of stride include Fats Waller and Art Tatum. Waller gained a reputation for his supple touch on the piano, his skills as an entertainer, and as the author or coauthor of classics like "Honeysuckle Rose" and "Ain't Misbehavin'." Besides an active recording career during the 1920s, he worked with lyricists Andy Razaf on three Broadway shows, *Keep Shufflin'*, *Load of Coal*, and *Hot Chocolates*. If Waller was known for his subtlety, then Tatum was known for his technical agility. Tatum was capable of performing so quickly, critics noted, that he generated a sound that sometimes reminded listeners of three pianos instead of one. The versatility of both pianists expanded the role of the piano, suggesting larger ensembles that began appearing during the latter half of the 1920s and early 1930s.

The Cotton Club

A number of these early, large jazz bands appeared in Harlem nightclubs. The Cotton Club was not only the best-known nightspot in Harlem during the 1920s and 1930s, it also was the best-known nightspot in all of New York City. The club was opened by Owney Madden in 1922 and served as a front for selling illegal bootleg liquor through the Prohibition era. The nightclub's exotic floor shows were reminiscent of minstrel shows from the nineteenth century, featuring light-skinned black women as exotic dancers. An advertisement for the Cotton Club underlined its features: "Join the crowds after the theatre, all Broadway comes to Harlem. An eyeful of beauty! An earful of dance-compelling music! A mouthful of tasty food! Altogether a fine frolic for you!"[44] These dancers were supported by a big band, which was also responsible for creating original, jazz-oriented material for nightly performances.

Prominent African American musicians performed at the Cotton Club, including Duke Ellington, Cab Calloway, and Ethel Waters. Ellington established his reputation at the Cotton Club between 1927 and 1931, polishing his skills as a budding bandleader and as a composition writer. The nightspot opened at 10 P.M. and remained open until 3 A.M., Tuesday through Sunday, accommodating as many as seven hundred customers nightly. Typically, the clientele was made up of white, well-to-do New Yorkers out for a night on the town, and establishments like the Cotton Club were referred to as Black and Tans, meaning black entertainment for a white audience.

While the Cotton Club allowed Ellington and others to develop their talent, critics charged that the club excluded black clientele and reinforced black stereotypes with its floor shows. When the club was first open, blacks were barred from the club, with the exception of celebrities like dancer Bill "Bojangles" Robinson or singer Waters. The performers at the club were not allowed to eat or socialize at the establishment. Even when the Cotton Club changed its policy to allow blacks in, few blacks could afford the high admission price. Jazz historian Gioia writes, "The procurement of black entertainment for white audiences soon became, inevitably and fortuitously, a mini-industry, a burgeoning microcosm [miniature representation] of New York nightlife as a whole."[45]

The other complaint was focused on the floor show itself, which featured light-skinned blacks in exotic performances in

The hottest nightclub in New York City during the 1920s and 1930s was Harlem's Cotton Club. Duke Ellington, Cab Calloway, and Ethel Waters played there regularly.

sets designed to look like the African jungle. To critics, depicting blacks as exotic creatures from the remote jungles of Africa created broad and unfair stereotypes.

While these problems were regrettable, Ellington biographer John Edward Hasse underlines the symbolic importance of the Cotton Club to African Americans during the 1920s and 1930s:

> On a deeper level, the Cotton Club served as a safe haven, however highly stylized and restricted, for whites to encounter aspects of black *culture*. In a decade when the Ku Klux Klan was nationally resurgent, and opportunities for whites to encounter blacks were circumscribed [limited] in many

ways, the Cotton Club provided a view of black Americans as handsome, accomplished, gifted, and yes, elegant. That view was highly stylized and limited: the African-Americans at the Cotton Club—Ellington included—all wore invisible theatrical masks.[46]

In allowing a display for talented African American musicians and bandleaders, the Cotton Club essentially accomplished the same task for jazz that intellectuals had hoped the Harlem Renaissance would accomplish for black painters and novelists: The club offered a venue that highlighted black artistry.

The Birth of Big Bands

The stride players of rent parties and the big bands of the Cotton Club formed significant strands of a new development within jazz during the late 1920s and early 1930s. The shift from small combos like Louis Armstrong and King Oliver's Chicago bands in the mid-1920s to big band music in the 1930s was gradual. From the mid-to-late-1920s, Armstrong, Ellington, and others formed larger bands, but the focus of these bands remained on the solos of leading players. New developments in rhythm and arranging, however, were pushed forward by the demands of a broader public seeking quality entertainment. While a small number of the jazz audience may have been content to listen to a jazz band perform at the Cotton Club or other venues, many wanted to dance. In order to create dance music, bandleaders needed to find new ways to add rhythm and swing to jazz.

One of the keys to this shift was the role of the rhythm section within a big band, switching from two-four to four-four time. Two-four time created a quick, sometimes jerky rhythm, while four-four allowed for a slower, smoother rhythm to underpin a jazz band. Four-four time was partly made possible by the introduction of the acoustic, stand-up bass, which helped provide a smooth rhythm. This created a more flexible rhythm section in bands and raised the profiles of drummers, bassists, pianists, and rhythm guitarists. These musicians generated a forward-moving rhythm that served as a backdrop for multiple sections within big bands.

The other sections of a big band worked against this rhythmic backdrop. The saxophone, or woodwind, section included three to five saxophones, including alto, tenor, and sometimes baritone saxophones. Both the trumpet and the trombone sections also included three to five musicians. The inclusion of a full rhythm, saxophone, trumpet, and trombone section, along with the occasional additions of flutists and clarinetists, could easily create bands of over twenty players. Big bands, then, comprised a large number of musicians playing saxophones, trumpets, guitar, bass, trombones, clarinets, and drums.

Because of the size of a big band, an essential component to big band jazz was an arranger, a person who wrote charts for the

Big bands, such as Cab Calloway's, added the stand-up bass and guitar to the rhythm section and expanded the role of woodwind instruments to create a more complex but uncluttered jazz sound.

various instruments and sections of a band. With smaller combos of five to seven musicians, performers were able to retain an uncluttered sound. In larger bands, charts assigned harmony, counterparts, and lead roles to different musicians, assuring an orderly sound. An arranger's chart also helped a band achieve a unique style that separated it from other bands. One band, for instance, might rely on a big saxophone section, while another might replace part of the saxophone section with clarinets and flutes. While arrangers often worked behind the scenes, they became one of the most valuable assets of big bands during the 1930s and 1940s.

The use of charts also dictated a higher level of musicianship. Jazz historian John F. Szwed notes, "Swing was made possible by the substantial number of well-educated musicians in the United States who at this point could read or write sophisticated arrangements."[47]

Jazz musicians, like classical musicians, had to be able to read music in order to understand the charts. In the past, when a musician joined an established band he or she would have to learn all of the band's material. Now, a new musician simply had to be able to read charts. With a smoother rhythm section, and multiple players and arrangers, big band leaders were in a position to push jazz in new directions during the 1930s. The rise of big bands, however, faced one potential obstacle: Swing was born during the onset of the Great Depression.

The Great Depression and Big Bands

The rise of the big bands occurred during one of the worst financial crises in American history. The Great Depression was a bleak period in U.S. history that began after stock prices on New York's Wall Street, the financial center of the United States, fell to an all-time low in 1929. This crisis continued to impact the economic well-being of many Americans throughout the 1930s. Unemployment remained high, and many Americans had to depend on public assistance to survive. Nightclubs, like all businesses during the 1930s, struggled to attract customers, many of whom suffered from reduced incomes.

The rise of big bands, which required nightclubs to hire ten, fifteen, or more musicians at one time, seemed like an improb-

Billie Holiday's "Strange Fruit"

One of the most critically acclaimed jazz singers, Billie Holiday fronted a number of big bands during the 1930s and 1940s. In 1939, she introduced "Strange Fruit," a song fashioned from a poem by Lewis Allan. "Strange Fruit" was controversial because it directly addressed the subject of the lynching of blacks in the South. She later wrote about the song in her autobiography *Lady Sings the Blues*:

> It was during my stint at the Café Society that a song was born which became my personal protest—"Strange Fruit." The germ of the song was in a poem written by Lewis Allan. I first met him in the Café Society. When he showed me the poem, I dug it right off. . . .

> I was scared people would hate it ["Strange Fruit"]. The first time I sang it I thought it was a mistake and I had been right being scared. There wasn't even a patter of applause when I finished. Then a lone person began to clap nervously. Then suddenly everyone was clapping.

> It caught on after a while and people began to ask for it. The version I recorded for Commodore [a record label] became my biggest selling record. It still depresses me every time I sing it, though.

Billie Holiday. *Lady Sings the Blues.* New York: Broadway, 1956, pp. 94–95.

able development in the face of economic hardship. Many customers, after all, would have been unable to pay a cover charge for entering the nightclub. "With the Wall Street crash of 1929 and the rise of the Depression," notes jazz journalist Scott Yanow, "one would expect that big bands would have become less viable economically, but ironically the opposite occurred."[48] Despite the economic hardships of the era, big bands developed for at least two reasons. For one, the move toward playing for larger crowds required a bigger sound and since these larger crowds wanted to dance, they also required a swinging rhythm in which big bands specialized. The second element that made big bands practical was the end of Prohibition in 1934. Now nightclubs could legally serve alcohol, and the money made from the sale of drinks helped support the larger bands.

Despite the Depression, Americans continued to buy music, attend dance halls, and listen to big bands on the radio. As a result, big bands would become the most popular music in the United States between 1935 and 1946. Jazz historian Joachim Berendt writes:

> Soon, swing seemed to be everywhere. Live music could be heard from all parts of the country every night on radio, and people from different regions could hear musicians and styles previously limited to a local area. . . . By the early 1930s swing was firmly established as the pop music of America.[49]

Duke Ellington and Count Basie

Two of the most exciting bandleaders during the 1930s were Ellington and Count Basie. While both leaders gained reputations for their ability to attract quality sidemen for their orchestras, they nonetheless represented two different approaches to big band jazz. The complexity of Ellington's compositions created a rich tapestry of melody and rhythm; Basie, on the other hand, developed a simpler style, more heavily anchored in the blues.

When Ellington and his band opened at the Cotton Club in 1927, it was an important occasion in Harlem. Ellington had already established himself as a talented stride pianist, but his tenure at the Cotton Club provided a nightly education in operating a band. "He [Ellington] did not learn his art in a conservatory or with the encouragement of wealthy patrons," notes jazz historian John Fordham, "but as a Harlem bandleader, where the closest species to a patron was the mobster."[50] Following in the footsteps of jazz pioneer Jelly Roll Morton, Ellington became a prolific composer, penning "East St. Louis Toodle-oo," "Black and Tan Fantasy," and "Mood Indigo." In his arrangements, he wrote specific parts that highlighted longtime band members. While Ellington's band would never reach the popularity of bands led by white leaders like Benny Goodman, his creativity made him perhaps the most influential bandleader/composer of the big band era.

Duke Ellington's (left) style was a rich tapestry of melodies and rhythms while Count Basie (right) had a style more grounded in the blues. When they collaborated in 1961 they merged their styles on the album *First Time! The Count Meets the Duke.*

While the New York jazz scene expanded in Harlem night-clubs during the late 1920s, a lively scene also had developed in Kansas City. There, in the rough and tumble of Kansas City nightlife, pianist Basie developed a looser style than many big bands of the era. He added texture to his band's sound by developing a minimalistic piano style, mixing brief flourishes of notes with silence. "He [Basie] smoothed out the syncopated thump of stride," writes jazz historian Fordham, "and concentrated on a simple solo style, discreetly prompting the band."[51] On pieces like "Jumpin' at the Woodside" and the group's theme, "One O'Clock Jump," Basie's band generated rhythms that many other swing bands attempted to copy.

Both Ellington and Basie expanded the possibility of big band jazz during the 1930s and 1940s, and showcased the abilities of African American musicians for all Americans. As writers and in-

Charlie Christian

Charlie Christian was one of the first musicians to play electric guitar in a jazz setting. Before him, acoustic guitar had mostly served as a rhythm instrument, with the guitarist playing chords behind lead instruments. Partly, this use of the guitar came from tradition, but the guitar was also limited because of its low volume in public performances. Amplifiers, modifying the guitar sound to a louder level, allowed the player to perform lead parts, just like a trumpet and saxophone player. In the following passage, jazz writer Bill Simon speaks of Christian's legacy:

> Charlie Christian probably is the only jazz figure who would have been able to serve as a model stylist on his chosen instrument as long as fifteen years after his disappearance from the scene. There isn't an important guitarist playing today who does not recognize him as the all-time best, and who does not credit him as a prime influence. In most of the better modernists, the strain has crossed with that of saxophonist, Charlie Parker, but basically, it's Charlie Christian. The best thing anyone can say about a guitarist today is that he could be "the closest thing to Christian."

James Sallis, ed. *Jazz Guitars: An Anthology*. New York: Quill, 1984, p. 117.

novators, they built on and expanded earlier jazz traditions. Ellington's compositional style even expanded beyond jazz, leading to comparisons between *Black, Brown and Beige* and works by classical musicians. While jazz musicians were often unschooled in the early years of the music's development, Ellington and Basie created rich bodies of work that gave witness to a new level of African American artistry.

Chapter Four

The Bebop Revolution and Beyond (mid-1940s–1958)

If jazz had seemed to progress in an orderly fashion through the mid-1940s, with styles reflecting influences from New Orleans, Chicago, and New York City, changes after World War II would be less easy to trace. The changes occurred more rapidly, as did the changes within popular culture as a whole. The revolutionary bebop would quickly be followed by the jazz styles known as East Coast, cool, West Coast, and hard bop, among others.

The variety of jazz styles developed during this era sometimes had racial overtones. Many West Coast and cool jazz performers were white, while the majority of hard bop, funk, and East Coast musicians were black. While these overtones often seemed to split different styles into white jazz and black jazz, most styles included both black and white players. While cool jazz included many white players like trumpeter Chet Baker, for instance, African American Miles Davis was perhaps the biggest influence within the emergence of the West Coast style, a mainly white-influenced style of jazz.

These transitions in jazz would continue to take place against a backdrop of the black experience in post–World War II America. While most white Americans experienced prosperity following World War II, many blacks continued to struggle for economic and social equality. This struggle also underpinned the outlook of many African American jazz performers.

By the mid-1940s, African American jazz artists began making a connection between jazz as art and politics. While many black musicians had been able to earn a living playing big band music, they frequently earned less than whites. Furthermore, a number of African American musicians found the popular swing music repetitive and nonartistic. "They were bored, talented and rebellious," notes jazz historian John Fordham, "and they lived for playing."[52] More and more, black musicians believed they needed to find a new, less-worn path to create jazz art. Within this expression, black musicians attempted to form a new freedom through music.

Bebop Is Born

It is difficult to understand how different bebop sounded to listeners when it first appeared on the jazz scene in 1945–1946. "Many of the leading swing musicians of the 1940s," writes Fordham, "felt personally insulted."[53] While a number of established swing musicians like saxophonist Coleman Hawkins and pianist Art Tatum were able to adjust to bebop, most who pursued bebop were young musicians who had grown bored with big band jazz. Originally, young players like saxophonist Charlie Parker, trumpeter Dizzy Gillespie, and many others met after hours at clubs like Minton's Playhouse in Harlem. In these clubs, they jammed and experimented, trying new ideas and taking musical chances.

The most obvious change between swing and bebop was the size of the bands. While swing had used small orchestras of twelve or more musicians, bebop preferred small combos of four to six players. Few beboppers played clarinet or rhythm guitar, and arrangers, central to big band jazz, were less important in bepob. Bebop bands preferred upbeat tempos, and musicians delivered complex solos filled with chord changes and rich melodies. If

Trumpeter Dizzy Gillespie (far right) was one of the early Bebop musicians. Bebop was born from late-night experimental jams and extended the limits of conventional jazz.

big band jazz arrangements sometimes created music that seemed conventional, bebop strived for revelation and surprise. Jazz instructor Mark Gridley describes bebop in relation to Gillespie and Parker's recording of "Shaw Nuff":

> The sound of bop is often incomprehensible to listeners the first few times they hear it. The contours of the phrases are jagged with unexpected accents and frequent changes in direction. The improvisers pack their solos with many different melodic ideas in rapid succession. Because of this, audiences often perceive the music as chaotic. But bop becomes

more comprehensible as it becomes more familiar, and we can easily familiarize ourselves with it by replaying recordings. Just as a foreign language becomes less forbidding as we begin to recognize its words, bop becomes more comprehensible as we begin to recognize its standard accompaniment devices and we begin to partition the solo improvisations according to those markers. After listening only a few times to a piece, we can begin to recognize phrases and follow the contours of the solos.[54]

Minton's Playhouse

Minton's Playhouse in Harlem was perhaps the central nightclub where bebop developed. In his memoirs, Dizzy Gillespie recalls performing at Minton's during the mid-1940s:

> What happened down at Minton's anyway? On Monday nights, we used to have a ball. Everybody from the Apollo [another nightclub], on Monday nights, was a guest at Minton's, the whole band. We had a big jam session. Monday night was the big night, the musician's night off. There was always some food there for you. Oh, that part was beautiful. Teddy Hill [Minton's manager] treated the guys well. He didn't pay much money—I never did get paid— but he treated the guys nicely. There was always some food there for you. He had a kitchen, you know, and you could eat there. . . .

> What we were doing at Minton's was playing, seriously creating a new dialogue among ourselves, blending our ideas into a new style of music. You only have so many notes, and what makes a style is how you get from one note to the other. We had some fundamental background training in European harmony and music theory superimposed on our own knowledge from Afro-American musical tradition. We invented our own way of getting from one place to the next.

Dizzy Gillespie. *To Be or Not to Bop: Memoirs—Dizzy Gillespie.* Garden City, NY: Doubleday, 1979, pp. 139–41.

It has been suggested that one of the reasons that bebop shocked listeners was the gap in new music following a recording ban during World War II. During the war, a disagreement between radio owners and a musicians' union led to a ban on new recordings. Because of this, it has been argued, few people were able to hear the early experiments that led to bebop. "Bebop musicians honed the music almost in secret as far as the mainstream record-buying public was aware,"[55] notes Fordham. As a result, when the first records were issued, bebop, as a new form of jazz, was fully developed. With its quickness of chord changes, the angularity of the solos, and the harmonic interplay of two or more musicians, bebop sounded nothing like big band jazz.

By rejecting the big band sound and adapting a noncommercial attitude toward music, black musicians were also rebelling against their status within American culture. During the 1930s and 1940s, a number of black musicians had been able to make more money by performing with white bands than black. Even then, however, these musicians were sometimes not allowed to eat at the same restaurants or sleep in the same hotels as their bandmates. Within bebop, black musicians inserted cultural influences. Some of these influences derived from Africa and the Caribbean, and a number of musicians expressed an interest in Islam, a key African religion. As an expression of culture, bebop drew deeply from the black experience and refused to compromise.

Charlie Parker and Dizzy Gillespie

While a number of musicians contributed to the rise of bebop, none held more importance to the movement than saxophonist Parker. Parker began playing the saxophone as a teenager and was influenced by saxophonist Lester Young, who had played in Basie's band. By the early-to-mid-1940s, however, Parker moved away from swing, fashioning a new, insistent technique of playing jazz saxophone. He played at a frantic pace, doubling and even quadrupling his timing, and never seemed to run out of ideas when soloing. "Jazz musicians and historians," writes Gridley, "feel that he is the most important saxophonist in jazz history. Many musicologists consider Parker one of the most brilliant musical figures in the twentieth century."[56] Parker also wrote a

Charlie Parker

Charlie Parker was perhaps the most influential jazz performer of his era and one of the most influential in all of jazz. In the following passage, Ira Gitler remembers Parker, known to many by his nickname, Bird.

Bird was a warm person, sensitive to public reaction. I remember talking to him one night at the Three Deuces [a nightclub] in the summer of 1947, just after he returned from a seven-month confinement at Camarillo State Hospital in California, where he had recuperated from a nervous collapse. He stressed the fact that "the young people are getting with the music." It seemed very important to him to communicate the spirit of jazz to the next generation. For his music came from the very roots of jazz and always possessed its basic elements, no matter how oblique his flights may have seemed. His awareness of the entire jazz literature can be heard in his quote from Louis Armstrong's *West End Blues* in his own *Visa* solo from *Bird at St. Nicks*.

Parker was a giant figure who influenced countless lives, musically and otherwise. He affected jazz as totally as had Armstrong a generation before him, and he brought the alto saxophone to prominence the way Coleman Hawkins and Lester Young had with the tenor saxophone. Because of him, young musicians turned to the alto and tried to play like him.

Ira Gitler. *The Masters of Bebop: A Listener's Guide.* New York: Da Capo, 2001, pp. 15–16.

Alto-saxophonist Charlie Parker was nicknamed Bird for his "flights" of improvisation while playing.

number of compositions including "Billie's Bounce," "Now's the Time," and "Confirmation." Despite his brilliance as a musician, Parker was also plagued by many personal problems, including drug addiction, and he died at the age of thirty-four in 1955.

Gillespie was the preeminent bebop trumpeter, reaching and holding higher notes longer than earlier jazz masters. Early in his career, he was influenced by big band performers like trumpeter Roy Eldridge, but by the early-to-mid-1940s, he had developed his own style. "Dizzy Gillespie's harmonic skills were startling, and he flaunted them," states Gridley. "His phrases were full of surprises and playful changes of direction."[57] Gillespie was an innovator even beyond bebop. He experimented with Latin music, combining bebop with Cuban rhythms, and also wrote bebop arrangements for big bands. His compositions "A Night in Tunisia" and "Groovin' High" became jazz standards.

While Parker and Gillespie were joined by many other players on the bebop scene during the mid-1940s, each musician's compositions, recordings, and live performances from this era served to signal the rise of a new generation of performers and the prominence of bebop.

From Cool Jazz to West Coast

In many ways, cool jazz was seen as a reaction to bebop. While cool jazz embraced a number of bebop's stylistic alterations, it also softened the angular edges of these alterations. "Bop was furious, fast and hot," writes jazz chronicler Martin Gayford. "Cool was less emotionally engaged, more melodic, lighter in feel."[58] To the innovators who first played cool, however, it was simply another way of expanding how jazz could be played. If beboppers argued that big bands had limited artistic expression, other musicians argued that bebop limited artistic expression in another way. Because bebop used popular songs for the base of a soloist's flight, the structures of these songs hemmed in a performer's options. By combining swing and bebop, cool jazz created a sophisticated blend that relied on written arrangements, collective instrumental parts, and light-toned solo work. The musician most responsible for initiating these changes and jump starting the new movement was trumpeter Davis.

Miles Davis (standing) plays trumpet as accompanying musicians record a song for Davis's legendary album *Birth of the Cool.*

Davis embarked on a number of studio sessions in 1949–1950 with a nine-piece band and arranger Gil Evans, and these recordings would form the foundation of cool jazz. Evans drew inspiration from multiple musical sources, from Duke Ellington to the European classical tradition, and Davis chose performers who focused on carefully measured solos. The result was *Birth of the Cool*, and jazz writer John F. Szwed describes one song from the session:

"Move" (1949) has the tightly coiled, jaggedly wired melody line of a bebop tune and wears its rhythm up front. . . . But this arrangement by John Lewis softens the edges by its voicings and light phrasing, and by the introduction of a tranquil countermelody. It was a 78-rpm single with only three minutes to play with, but everyone makes the most of it. Davis's solo is concise and to the point. . . . There is a residue of big band conventions in the passage surrounding Max Roach's drum breaks, but the independent tuba line, the interplay of the horns, and the restraint of the rhythm section all signaled that an alternative to the big band was in the air.[59]

Many people involved in the *Birth of the Cool* sessions became leading practitioners of cool and West Coast jazz.

Cool jazz sometimes overlapped with West Coast jazz, becoming West Coast cool, and both critics and fans have often used these terms interchangeably. More than cool jazz, West Coast

Bebop Criticized

Bebop was criticized by both jazz writers and established jazz musicians. "The sounds of bop were literally unheard of, and accordingly, controversial," noted an early jazz chronicler, Marshall W. Stearns in *The Story of Jazz*. Trumpeter Louis Armstrong, a trendsetter during the 1920s, offered his own view of the new music:

> They [the beboppers] want to carve everyone else because they're full of malice, and all they want to do is show you up, and any old way will do as long as it's different from the way you played it before. So you get all them weird chords which don't mean nothing, and first people get curious about it just because it's new, but soon they get tired of it because it's really no good and you got no melody to remember and no beat to dance to. So they're all poor again and nobody is working, and that's what the modern malice done for you.

Quoted in Marshall W. Stearns, *The Story of Jazz*. New York: Oxford University Press, 1956, p. 219.

served as a convenient label for musicians and record labels active in Los Angeles and surrounding areas. Also, the label was adapted when *Life* magazine featured a story on trumpeter Baker and the Gerry Mulligan Quartet. Both the *Life* piece and the marketing labels gave the impression that West Coast jazz was a unified movement. This impression, however, was only partly true. "If the music was easy to label," notes historian Szwed, "when looked at in retrospect it is another case of a variety of styles being treated as if they were one."[60]

Cool jazz and West Coast jazz were often seen as white jazz while bebop was seen as black jazz. This division, however, was never completely true. Davis was perhaps the most influential innovator within cool jazz, and a number of black musicians played cool and West Coast jazz. Also, one of the most influential musicians within cool jazz was Basie's saxophonist, Young. Despite these crossovers, many jazz fans and journalists continued to perceive these divisions of jazz styles as separations between white and black players.

Hard Bop

If cool and West Coast jazz were seen as a reaction to bebop, then hard bop was seen as a reaction to cool. Hard bop, however, was also a response to the overwhelming popularity of the latest music craze of the mid-1950s, rock and roll, which attracted a large, young audience. Like big band music, rock and roll was dance music, and it drew from the emotional current of the blues, rhythm and blues (R&B), and even jazz. Unlike the sometimes emotionally distant sounds of cool and West Coast jazz, rock and roll was exciting and passionate. According to jazz historian Fordham, "Rock made some of the routinely fashionable jazz of the early 1950s sound not just cool, but inert."[61] In response to cool jazz and rock and roll, hard bop wanted to reconnect jazz with the blues.

While bebop musicians often performed songs at a breakneck pace, hard bop musicians like trumpeter Clifford Brown, pianist Horace Silver, and saxophonist Sonny Rollins learned to vary tempos. Drummers like Max Roach and Art Blakey assumed central roles within the movement, pushing bands forward with propulsive, or forward-moving, rhythm. A number of musicians, including Jimmy Smith, Jimmy McGriff, and Shirley Scott, popularized the organ in jazz, often leading small combos and developing an offshoot to hard bop known as soul jazz. Jazz instructor Gridley lists several qualities of hard bop, including simpler improvised lines, more active drumming, darker musical tones, original compositions, smoother musical balance, hard-driving feeling, and a greater variety of rhythm.[62]

Hard bop drummer Art Blakey's style of propulsive rhythms was central to hard bop's driving force. Hard bop allowed drummers to become central to their bands' sound.

The majority of hard bop musicians found as little popularity as bebop musicians, and racial factors continued to influence how the music was perceived and how it was heard. If cool jazz was primarily located on the West Coast and its most popular performers had been white, then hard bop was primarily located in the eastern half of the United States, in cities like Detroit, and its best-known musicians were black. "If the music was coded black by listeners, some critics found it excessively so," notes jazz historian Szwed. "The English poet and conservative jazz critic Philip Larkin complained that the civil rights movement was destroying jazz."[63] Larkin and others worried that by drawing a connection between jazz and political freedom, blacks compromised the art of the music. Jazz, these critics believed, should be separate from political considerations. Despite its lack of popularity, and despite a backlash by some critics, hard bop nonetheless served to remind listeners and other musicians of jazz's roots.

Post Bop

As the musical careers of Thelonious Monk and Charles Mingus overlapped the bebop, cool, and hard bop movements, they performed music that remains difficult to classify. While these artists' early recordings often qualified as bebop, their work as leaders produced singular styles. In one sense, both performers were "musician's musicians," creating sometimes challenging work that other musicians studied.

Like many bebop players during the early 1940s, pianist Monk attended after-hours jam sessions in New York during the early-to-mid-1940s. "Monk was one of the most original of all jazz improvisers," notes Gridley. "In fact, his inventions sound so different from other styles that some listeners feel it is misleading to classify his style as swing or bop."[64] His exacting style, circling around a repeated phrase, could appear mathematical. Because Monk's solos mixed unusual chords, odd phrasings, and extended silence, only a small number of musicians were comfortably able to perform with him. Still, a number of Monk's compositions became popular standards, including "'Round Midnight" and "Straight, No Chaser."

Mingus represents a rare example of a jazz bass player who led his own bands. After working with a number of jazz greats in-

Pianist Thelonius Monk and stand-up bassist Charles Mingus jam with Charlie Parker (right) in New York in 1953. Both Monk and Mingus spanned the bebop, cool, and hard bop movements. Their later work would produce their own singular styles.

cluding classic jazz trumpeter Louis Armstrong, swing bandleader Ellington, and bebop saxophonist Parker, Mingus established himself within hard bop. Even within hard bop, however, he remained difficult to classify. "Mingus is typically seen," notes jazz historian Ted Gioia, "as a musician who defies category, a progressive who never really embraced the avant-garde, and a traditionalist who constantly tinkered with the legacies of the past."[65] As a composer, arranger, and musician, Mingus drew from gospel, the blues, and early jazz, but always reinterpreted these forms. On a piece like "Wednesday Night Prayer Meeting," his band re-created the evangelical excitement of a prayer meeting, holding a balance between New Orleans and more experimental forms of jazz.

So singular were Monk and Mingus's achievements, that their music remains easily identifiable. The influence of both musicians, through their compositional skills and the sidemen who worked in their bands, expanded jazz's horizons during the 1940s and 1950s. Monk and Mingus also recorded an impressive body of work that helped set the stage for further experimentation during the late 1950s.

Chapter Five

Free Jazz and Other Experiments (1959–1967)

Beginning with bebop in 1945–1946, jazz styles began to change more rapidly and they frequently overlapped with one another. This trend continued in 1959 with the development of at least three recognizable styles: mainstream, modal, and free jazz. Over the next several years, these styles would be joined by Latin, bossa nova, and third-stream jazz. As in the past, a number of personalities drove the new music forward, including Miles Davis, John Coltrane, and Ornette Coleman. Unlike earlier eras, however, many musicians moved between different categories of jazz, making Davis, Coltrane, and others difficult to classify. All of these changes, both evolutions and revolutions within jazz, would also take place beside an expanding civil rights movement during the 1950s and 1960s.

The civil rights movement enriched these developments and formed an essential backdrop for jazz musicians. Even while jazz was often performed without sung lyrics, the music frequently represented African American aspirations for equality in

Ella Fitzgerald performs at a nightclub in 1958. Many claim she had a beautiful voice with a wide range that could shatter glass, and she was a brilliant scat singer with near-perfect elocution.

the United States. Even in the late 1950s and early 1960s, many blacks were still denied basic rights in the Southern United States. Many blacks and whites joined the civil rights movement, marching and speaking out against injustice to blacks and other minorities, while others expressed their support for the movement through their music. For a small group of adventurous musicians during the late 1950s and early 1960s, there was no difference between expressing political views and performing jazz. To them, jazz expression was political expression.

As musicians and as Americans, blacks had long hoped to achieve the same economic, social, and artistic status as all Americans. During the late and early 1960s, the desire for equality became more assertive and, at times, less willing to compromise. This assertiveness was present in lunch counter sit-ins in the South, in which blacks sat in whites-only seats and refused to leave, as well as in the cry of a horn in a free jazz concert in downtown New York. No matter what the means of expression, African Americans were no longer willing to be treated as second-class citizens.

Jazz in the Mainstream

As jazz became more experimental during the late 1950s, a number of musicians offered recordings that maintained the status quo or maintained what some critics thought of as the mainstream. Sometimes these were established musicians like Duke Ellington and Louis Armstrong, who continued to record in an older style. Even while big band music no longer sustained its popularity, many performers continued to work and record in smaller groups appealing to older jazz fans who had never adjusted to bebop and newer fans who appreciated the more melodic, older style. According to jazz historian John Fordham:

> They [swing musicians] may have been out of the head-lines, but given a chance, the swing stars still produced performances brimming with all the old prebop virtues of relaxed, loping rhythms, conversational solos, accessible, songlike themes, and a lot of blues, and the mixture began to find a new audience.[66]

A number of jazz vocalists also worked within the mainstream. In 1958, on the verge of multiple changes within jazz, singer Ella Fitzgerald issued *Ella Fitzgerald Sings the Irving Berlin Song Book*, an album in an ongoing series in which she recorded the work of major songwriters from the 1930s and 1940s. "Blessed with a beautiful voice and a wide range," notes jazz journalist Scott Yanow, "Ella could out swing anyone, was a brilliant scat singer and had near-perfect elocution; one could always understand the words she sang."[67] Also in 1958, vocalist Sarah Vaughan recorded *No Count Sarah* with Count Basie, including versions of Irving Berlin's "Cheek to Cheek" and Cole Porter's "Just One of Those Things." Other singers of the era included Billie Holiday and Carmen McRae.

During the 1950s, critic Stanley Dance also identified a style of jazz that he called mainstream. Dance saw mainstream jazz as falling between bebop and revival styles like Dixieland, similar to big band jazz, but played in smaller groups. A number of the musicians who performed in the mainstream style had worked during the 1930s and 1940s, like trumpeter Buck Clayton, tenor saxophonist Zoot Sims, and pianist Erroll Garner. These musicians retained an allegiance to jazz and pop standards from the 1930s and 1940s. Over time, however, even Dance realized that older styles, including the once radical bebop, eventually became accepted as mainstream.

Free Jazz

If many listeners accepted the easy-flowing sounds of mainstream and traditional jazz at the end of the 1950s, free jazz often experienced a much more hostile reception. Historically, free jazz represented the biggest break in jazz styles since bebop in the mid-1940s. Unlike bebop, however, free jazz deviated even further from a style that would be recognized as jazz, eliminating conventional boundaries in the process. Paradoxically, many free jazz players expressed a desire to return to the basics, even beyond the beginnings of jazz. According to jazz chronicler Martin Gayford, "The new music—the New Thing, as it was sometimes called—was arguably a sort of return to more purely African roots, jettisoning [abandoning] the European elements of jazz: conventional harmony and form."[68]

Traditional rules, in the hands of musicians and composers like pianist Cecil Taylor, saxophonist Coleman, and pianist Sun Ra, were broken. This disregard of familiar boundaries and a search for deeper roots made many critics, fans, and musicians angry. These fans expected musicians to uphold tradition or to explore tradition in a more acceptable way. To these fans, free jazz was not really jazz at all.

In one sense, however, the very term *free jazz* was confusing. It insinuated that there were no boundaries at all, that jazz players no longer used chords, riffs, and melody, and that all structure had been discarded. While many traditional elements were put aside, the degree of displacement depended upon the particular musician and even then, could shift from recording to recording. In general, free jazz bands eliminated the pianist, the person most responsible for playing background chords to guide the other musicians. Many free jazz musicians also extended the conventional range of their instruments, especially horn players. A saxophonist, for instance, could push the pitch of his horn, eliciting shrieks and honks, sounds that would have been considered noises in

From Dixieland to Free Jazz

While many critics and musicians viewed free jazz as having little connection to traditional jazz, drummer Milford Graves recalls how Dixieland led him to the new music:

> I have to say it was Dixieland that led me to free. It was really the only kind of music I knew inside out apart from the marching band music I grew up with as a kid. Compared to most bop, Dixieland is very free. Bop is an extremely disciplined music, but there was a lotta stuff in the kind of Dixieland I played that was really wide open. I loved the fact that if you played one of the instruments in the band you had a part to play. You'd learn what to do from masters who played the traditional trombone or clarinet roles in creating the texture in the music. Once you had your part, you had a stepping stone for your improvisation. I loved the way that Dixieland musicians improvised collectively. So in free jazz, I was coming from that a lot of the time.

Quoted in Alyn Shipton, *A New History of Jazz*. New York: Continuum, 2008, p. 799.

the past. While free jazz did not eliminate every established rule, many free jazz players did push the limits of tradition further than they had ever been pushed.

Much of the controversy in 1959 centered on Coleman, especially his early recordings, *Tomorrow Is the Question* and *The Shape of Jazz to Come*, and his initial appearance at the Five Spot in New York City on November 17, 1959. In particular, the opening at the Five Spot was highly anticipated. Journalist A.B. Spellman notes the split within jazz in the wake of Coleman's music:

> The impact the Ornette Coleman quartet had in 1959 was cathartic. Musicians split into two camps—those who found this group incompetent and those who thought them revolutionary. It was not so much the substance of their music as it was the process. There was an obvious element of freedom in this group that existed in few others.[69]

While the shows at the Five Spot were well attended, audience members—like musicians—were split on the music: They either loved it or hated it.

Coleman's recordings continued to push the envelope on how far free jazz could go. The release of *Free Jazz* in 1960 proved as controversial as his band's performances at the Five Spot. For the session, Coleman gathered two quartets in the studio to record one composition, the thirty-seven-minute "Free Jazz." On the recording, each quartet is featured on one side of the stereo spectrum; after one quartet plays, the other responds. "There is an opening melody, a steady pulse and loose but organized parts between the solos," writes jazz journalist Yanow. "Otherwise this music . . . is completely free."[70] While free jazz never attained wide popularity, many of the innovations of the late 1950s and early 1960s would be measured against it.

Saxophonist Ornette Coleman and trumpeter Don Cherry trade notes at the Five Spot Café on November 7, 1958. Coleman's free-form style was highly controversial. Jazz fans either loved or hated it.

Modal Jazz

One of those innovations was modal jazz. Modal jazz was built on the concept of simplifying jazz's underlying structures by creating a detached backdrop of modes, or scales, that allowed musicians more freedom when soloing. Instead of jumping from one chord to the next, as bebop had done, modes relied on the looser backdrop of seven scales. Once a scale was chosen, musicians could develop solos without the clutter of continual chord changes. On the surface, modal jazz seemed similar to cool jazz, offering a mellower version of bebop. Cool jazz, however, continued to use traditional chord sequences as typified in popular songs, which meant that the musicians had to follow the logic of continuous chord changes. With modes, a jazz group simply decided the number of measures that they would extend each mode; liberated from chord changes, the soloist could float inside the free space. Arriving in 1959, modal jazz also offered an alternative to other jazz trends. According to jazz historian Fordham, "Modalism offered a more accessible alternative to free music in loosening jazz structure, although many players chose to use combinations of old and new forms."[71]

The album that served to introduce the jazz world to the new form in 1959 was Davis's *Kind of Blue*, one of the most popular jazz albums of all time. Davis gathered pianist Bill Evans, saxophonists Coltrane and Cannonball Adderley, drummer Jimmy Cobb, and bassist Paul Chambers. Pianist Wynton Kelly would also play on one track. As was common of many jazz albums at the time, *Kind of Blue* was taped quickly in two recording sessions, and the album was pressed and issued only four months after the recording. While critical reaction to *Kind of Blue* was positive, Davis and modal jazz was somewhat overshadowed at the time by the work of Coleman and other musicians working within free jazz.

Jazz journalist Ashley Kahn notes two primary changes that modal jazz initiated. First, compositions were played at slower tempos, allowing the musicians room to develop their sound, or solo style. The second characteristic evolved from the slower tempos, with musicians playing longer solos. "Loosed from the traditional thirty-two or twelve-bar song structure," writes Kahn,

Kind of Blue

———————— ■ ————————

In the following excerpt, journalist Ashley Kahn recalls entering the studio to listen to the original tapes for *Kind of Blue*. Conducting research for a book on the 1959 album, he anticipated what he would hear:

> The tape threaded its way across the playback heads and I heard the voices of Miles Davis and his producer, Irving Townsend, the instantly recognizable sound of Miles's trumpet, John Coltrane's tenor, Cannonball Adderley's alto and the other musicians. I listened to their harmonized riffs start and stop and grew acclimated to the rhythm of the recording process. A few engineers who had heard that the masters were being played that day dropped by and quietly pulled up chairs or stood in the corner to listen. . . .
>
> As the first full take of "Freddie Freeloader" began playing, I put down my pen and focused on the music. By the time Coltrane began soloing, I was transported to an austere twilight world that requested silence and contemplation. I was familiar with the album from years of dedicated listening but the music's seductive spell had not lessoned—it still held the power to quiet all around it.

Ashley Kahn. *Kind of Blue: The Making of the Miles Davis Masterpiece*. New York: Da Capo, 2000, p. 16.

"the soloist was free to invent and reinvent as long as necessary to tell the story."[72] Unlike the earlier, more frantic bebop, modal jazz was often leisurely, more relaxed, and freer in structure.

As with *Kind of Blue*, these developments were reflected in other modal jazz recordings of the time. In 1961 saxophonist Coltrane issued *My Favorite Things*, an album that found him transforming from hard bop to modal jazz. The album contained only four recordings, including a thirteen-minute, forty-one-second version of the pop standard "My Favorite Things." "The session indicated scope for extended, trancelike improvising,"[73] writes jazz historian Fordham. Even during the early-to-mid-1960s, new musicians continued to work within the modal jazz style. These included pianist Herbie Hancock, who recorded *Maiden Voyage* in 1965 and would later work with Davis, and pianist McCoy Tyner, who issued *The Real McCoy* in 1967.

Other Jazz

The development of Latin jazz and bossa nova became popular during the early 1960s. Latin influences had entered the work of musicians like trumpeter Dizzy Gillespie in the late 1940s, and musicians like Mongo Santamaria emerged in the late 1950s with albums like *Mongo*. Bossa nova developed in Brazil during the mid-to-late-1950s and emerged in the United States in 1962 with the release of Stan Getz and Charlie Byrd's *Jazz Samba*. Jazz journalist Richard S. Ginell writes, "A fresh breeze of warm South American air blew through American jazz in the early 1960s, the seductive blend of Brazilian rhythms, American cool jazz, and advanced European classical harmony that became known as bossa nova."[74]

Bossa nova combined the sounds of cool jazz with Brazilian rhythms, generating a quiet music with easy-flowing tempos and unusual musical signatures. The craze only lasted a short time, but during that time, many musicians were influenced by bossa nova. Even those who usually worked in other jazz fields chose to record albums in the bossa nova style. The general interest in merging different sounds and styles of music during this era also extended to third-stream jazz.

The idea of third-stream jazz was not a new idea in 1959, but an ongoing exploration of ways to combine jazz with classical music that gained a new currency during this time. While classical composers had borrowed from jazz during an earlier period, most of the experimentation during the 1950s and 1960s found jazz musicians drawing from the classical tradition. An early example of third-stream jazz was the Modern Jazz Quartet's album *Third Stream Music*, recorded in 1960. Several songs from the album included the addition of a string quartet, adding a classical backing to jazz compositions. Another good example of this synthesis is Davis's recordings with arranger Gil Evans, specifically the team's work on sections of *Sketches of Spain* in 1960. As with the *Birth of the Cool* sessions, Davis and Evans carefully arranged lead trumpet and a larger orchestra to create a synthesis of European and African American sounds.

Latin, South American, and European influences blended with the more traditional influences during the late 1950s and early 1960s, enriching and broadening jazz. In a sense, this growth made jazz truly an international phenomenon. Early in the history of jazz, musicians had traveled to Europe and other locales to introduce the new American music. Now, jazz was drawing from world music, creating music that was global in scope and increasingly more difficult to classify.

The blending of Brazilian rhythms with jazz developed into the genre of bossa nova, which was best exemplified by percussionist Mongo Santamaria.

Civil Rights and Jazz

All of these developments in jazz took place against a backdrop of the civil rights movement during the 1950s and 1960s. Civil rights had been an ongoing concern in African American communities throughout the United States, but this concern intensified following the landmark Supreme Court decision *Brown v. Board of Education of Topeka, Kansas* in 1954, which ended state-sanctioned school segregation. In 1955 a bus boycott began in Montgomery, Alabama, with blacks refusing to ride on the city's segregated buses. The Montgomery movement also gave rise to the leadership of Martin Luther King Jr., a central voice in the ongoing struggle. "The bus boycott achieved remarkable solidarity," notes American historian George Brown Tindall. "Blacks in Montgomery formed car pools, hitchhiked, or simply walked."[75] With the ruling in *Brown v. Board of Education*, the desegregation of public schools began, and in 1957 U.S. president Dwight D. Eisenhower famously had to send in the National Guard to protect African American students attending a formerly all-white public school in Little Rock, Arkansas.

The residue of many of these events, underlining the need for greater equality and freedom, filtered into all aspects of African American culture, including black music from soul to jazz. According to jazz historian Ted Gioia:

> "Freedom" stood out as a politically charged word in American public discourse during the late 1950s and early 1960s—it would be hard, in fact, to find a term more explosive, more laden with depths of meaning, or proclaimed with more emotion during these tumultuous years. This one-time truism of civics classes and refrain from the nation's founding documents now took on new force, in the process outlining a sharp divide in the country's social and economic structures. The civil rights movement of the day raised it aloft as a battle cry, held it forth as a goal, and asserted it as a first principle on which all else depended. It could no longer be put out of mind as an empty phrase or accepted as a fiat accompli [an accomplished fact] in America society. "Freedom" was very much something to live for, or, for a few, even to die for.[76]

Sun Ra

Bandleader Sun Ra was one of the most creative and eccentric figures within jazz. He delved into electronics before many other jazz musicians and established his own record label. As with free jazz, the music that Sun Ra and his band recorded was adventurous and difficult to classify. His classification was further complicated by the sheer volume of his recordings: It is estimated that Sun Ra recorded over one hundred full-length albums. Sun Ra's eccentricity extended to his live shows.

In the following excerpt, jazz historian John F. Szwed describes the mixture of culture, music, and eccentricity that formed part of a live Sun Ra performance:

> His [Sun Ra's] six hour multimedia barrages could be genuinely frightening experiences. The music moved from stasis to chaos and back again, with shrieks and howls pouring out of what he called his Arkestra, whose members were dressed like archers of Arboria (from Buck Rogers). Dancers swirled through the audience; fire-eaters, gilded musclemen, and midgets paraded in front of masks, shadow puppets, and films of the pyramids. Nothing like it had been seen since [composer Richard] Wagner's spectacles at Bayreuth. Somehow Sun Ra's shows seemed to capture all the promise and the threat of the '60s—especially since no one in the audience had a clue as to what was going on. Sun Ra was jazz's great Romantic, who, like the great Romantics who preceded him in European music, understood that music could symbolize the unity in diversity that makes up the cosmos. But for him, the big band was his space vehicle, and African-American aesthetics his culture-synthesizing principle.

John F. Szwed. *Jazz 101: A Complete Guide to Learning and Loving Jazz*. New York: Hyperion, 2000, p. 237.

Sun Ra, left, plays piano onstage with his Arkestra. Sun Ra's style was so free flowing it was difficult to classify.

Freedom became the catchword of the era, and even the name of jazz albums—*Free Jazz*, *Free Form*, and *The Freedom Suite*—embraced the sentiment.

The politics of the era inspired and pushed pianist Taylor, saxophonist Coleman, and others forward into new territory. Reflecting on the civil rights movement during the late 1950s and early 1960s, many black jazz musicians refused to separate politics from music. Jazz, many musicians argued, was often limited by cultural constraints. One example was the longtime reliance within jazz on familiar pop songs. By relying on the structures of songs written for a broader, often white, audience, black performers had been forced to express their music within these perceived limitations.

Against a backdrop of the civil rights movement, these musicians were determined to abandon tradition for uncharted territory. For these musicians, free jazz offered more than a chance for artistic growth: Free jazz represented a deeply felt expression of black rebellion in America.

Miles Davis and John Coltrane

Two musicians who became caught up in the cultural and artistic changes of the era were Davis and Coltrane. Unlike Coleman and other free jazz players, Davis and Coltrane had been established within the jazz world for ten years by 1959. Both had also been involved in the birth of modal jazz in 1959, a music that many considered conservative compared to the free jazz of the same period. Both Davis and Coltrane, however, were also open to the new music, though their individual experiments with free jazz and post-bop would not take place until the mid-1960s.

During the mid-1960s Davis formed one of the most distinguished jazz quintets of the era, with pianist Hancock, bassist Ron Carter, drummer Tony Williams, and saxophonist Wayne Shorter. Between 1965 and 1968, the group recorded six albums that expanded modal jazz, leaving vast spaces for the musicians to interact with one another. Frequently referred to as post-bop, albums like *Nefertiti* (1967) and *Miles in the Sky* (1968) found a middle ground between free and structured jazz. Both drummer Williams and bassist Carter abandoned conventional rhythm structures, allowing the percussion and rhythm elements to perform a more interactive role with the other band members.

During this same time, Coltrane slowly transitioned from modal jazz to free form. In 1965 he recorded *Ascension* with ten other jazz players, including six horn players. "This historic

Early in his career, Herbie Hancock joined Miles Davis, Tony Williams, Ron Carter, and Wayne Shorter to record a series of albums that further expanded the limits of modal jazz. Hancock's success continued throughout the twentieth century.

outing can be looked at as John Coltrane's answer to Ornette Coleman's *Free Jazz* of four years earlier,"[77] writes jazz journalist Yanow. To many, the intensity of the music, with all of the saxophones and trumpets playing at once, was frightening. Coltrane continued to push these boundaries over the next two years, expanding the already open-ended music to the outer regions of what many considered to be jazz. By 1968, the year after Coltrane's death from liver cancer, these experiments were slowly being pushed to the side as new developments within jazz surfaced.

Chapter Six

Fusion and Beyond (1968–Present)

During the mid-to-late-1960s, a new movement in jazz once again seemed to turn many of the older jazz styles on their head. The surprising element of the newest style during the late 1960s was the role technology played. Whereas free jazz and other innovations had changed the way that jazz was played, jazz retained its basic instruments, such as saxophones, trumpets, bass, and drums. The addition of electricity, however, offered a new way of amplifying jazz and combining it with innovations borrowed from rock music. Combining jazz and rock, the innovative merger would be known as fusion. As with other changes in jazz, fusion also brought controversy, with critics claiming that fusion was not jazz.

In many ways the fusion movement, dominating jazz until the mid-1970s, would seemingly be the last of the observable changes or advances within jazz history. While the development of jazz had never been orderly, many historians found it easy to trace successive developments within jazz. For instance, New Orleans jazz had given way to big band jazz, which in turn gave way to bebop, free jazz, and, finally, fusion. It was easy for critics and fans who viewed these changes as progressive to worry over the fragmentation of jazz music and the fragmentation of jazz listeners. Looked at in a more positive light, however, these changes underlined a more pluralistic approach to jazz in which both old styles and new innovations were accepted under the broad umbrella of jazz.

This same pluralism also underpinned the black experience within America from the mid-1970s and beyond. Many blacks became interested in African roots and attempted to incorporate black heritage into everyday life. Simultaneously, the legal and social victories of the civil rights movement created new economic possibilities for blacks in America, establishing a less-segregated society. While many social problems remained

Guitarist John McLaughlin's Mahavishnu Orchestra fused jazz and rock to produce a unique sound.

for African Americans, and while racial harmony was less than perfect, the election of America's first black president, Barack Obama, in 2008 represented how far blacks had come since the birth of jazz in 1895.

Fusion

Like previous movements in jazz, there was never one style of fusion. The very word *fusion* seemed to capture the combination of rock and jazz, the merging of jazz with electricity. While jazz instruments had been amplified with electricity before, fusion seemed to push this element to the forefront, creating new roles for bassists, guitarists, and pianists. New instruments, the Rhodes electric piano and Moog synthesizer, allowed pianists to create rich textures, while amplification and special effects allowed guitarists to take a more central role within fusion bands.

Early on, fusion had been called jazz rock. For many jazz players, rock in the 1960s offered fresh possibilities, and a chance to re-energize what seemed—to a number of musicians—a form that was growing tired. Miles Davis and others listened to Sly and the Family Stone and Jimi Hendrix, and sometimes even performed in the same venues as rock artists during the late 1960s. Both the role of rhythm in rock along with the importance of the lead guitar player seeped into jazz. Likewise, jazz influenced many rock musicians during the late 1960s, with bands like Soft Machine and the Grateful Dead incorporating a number of jazz elements. The addition of electricity and the influence of rock were also evident in how this style of jazz was performed: With electrified instruments, groups like the Mahavishnu Orchestra could play as loudly as rock groups.

As had been true of many new movements in jazz since the late 1940s, trumpeter and bandleader Davis became the public face of the new music. As early as 1968, Davis's pianist, Herbie Hancock, began using an electric piano for *Filles de Kilimanjaro*, though the real change emerged at the beginning of 1969 with the release of *In a Silent Way*. "The beginning of fusion . . . ," notes jazz journalist Scott Yanow, "found Miles Davis for the first time really combining jazz improvising with the rhythms and power of rock."[78] This shift became more prominent—and public—with

Miles Davis led the way in the fusion genre with his seminal album *Bitches Brew*. Many session musicians from that recording went on to form their own fusion bands.

the release of *Bitches Brew* the same year. Music historian Chris Smith commented on the album:

> By the time *Bitches Brew* was released, Miles Davis was already a legend for pioneering both the "cool jazz" movement with his 1957 album *Birth of the Cool*, and the "modal jazz" genre with his 1959 release *Kind of Blue*. With *Bitches Brew*, Davis almost seemed to have jumped the jazz ship entirely, inspired by no less a rock god than Jimi Hendrix to escape the smooth, mellow tones he was known for by embracing an electric, heavily produced wall of sound that seemed geared more toward the massive psychedelic audience than the reserved jazz world. . . . Particularly on the twenty-six-minute title track and the overwhelming "Miles Runs the Voodoo Down," the listener can hear the powerful rock and funk that was coming out of 1960s' acts like James Brown and Sly and the Family Stone.[79]

Davis was joined by many others on the fusion scene, from young performers such as guitarist Larry Coryell to established players like trumpeter Donald Byrd.

By the early 1970s, fusion became popular as it splintered in a variety of directions. Most of the side players with Davis for the *Bitches Brew* sessions formed their own bands. Guitarist John McLaughlin formed the Mahavishnu Orchestra, drummer Tony Williams formed Tony Williams Lifetime, and Chick Corea formed Return to Forever. Ornette Coleman, a pioneer in free jazz during the 1960s, formed an electric band called Prime Time. Rock guitarist Carlos Santana also made fusion albums, including a joint effort with McLaughlin. As the movement entered the latter half of the 1970s, a number of mainstream fusion bands, such as the Yellow Jackets and Spyro Gyro, reached large audiences. Fusion, many believed, would only continue to grow.

Beyond Fusion

Despite the success of a number of mainstream fusion bands in the latter half of the 1970s, much of the ground that jazz had gained with the movement seemed to dissipate as the decade wore on. Part of fusion's fate was also wrapped up in the fate of rock music. By mid-decade, disco and other new forms of

Keith Jarrett

Pianist Keith Jarrett has been one of the most prolific and popular musicians in jazz since the 1970s. In the following excerpt, jazz historian John Fordham recaps Jarrett's many accomplishments:

> Pianist Keith Jarrett is one of the biggest box-office attractions in the jazz world. He records constantly, tours extensively, and improvises in the world's most prestigious concert halls under the most testing circumstances, unaccompanied or with only drums and bass. Jarrett refuses to be constrained by musical differences. A virtuoso pianist in any idiom, he has written symphonic works and recorded [Johann Sebastian] Bach on church organ and harpsichord. Some speculate that if [pianist Franz] Liszt had been born in the same time and place, this is how he would play. Jarrett's 1975 disk *The Köln Concert* is the best-selling solo piano record ever.

John Fordham. *Jazz: History, Instruments, Musicians, Recordings.* New York: Barnes and Noble, 1993, p. 123.

Pianist Keith Jarrett has written symphonic works as well as his own brand of jazz. He has been one of the most prolific and popular musicians in jazz since the 1970s.

music challenged rock's dominance of the radio and record-buying markets. As rock music faded from the mainstream, so did fusion.

That one kind of music could fade from the jazz scene was not unusual: This had happened many times in the past, as when big band jazz was replaced by other forms after World War II. What was unusual, however, was that fusion was not pushed out of the way by a new style during the late 1970s. Jazz journalist Yanow explains the situation:

> From 1915–75 the evolution of jazz moved remarkably fast as boundaries were broken and each style was a movement toward greater freedom and/or sophistication. From New Orleans jazz, classic jazz, Dixieland and swing to bop, cool jazz, hard bop, soul-jazz, free jazz and the avant-garde, the history moved quickly and logically. But after the intense and adventurous improvisers as pianist Cecil Taylor and tenor saxophonist Pharoah Sanders (in his early days) emerged, it became obvious that jazz could not get any freer. In fact, it could be said of tenor saxophonist Albert Ayler, whose music advanced from screaming sound explorations to early New Orleans–style marching bands, went so far ahead that he eventually came in at the beginning.[80]

Seemingly for the first time in jazz history, no single style emerged that served as a focal point for new development.

While no one style of jazz appeared, many jazz musicians who had been active during the 1960s and 1970s continued to perform and record during the 1980s and beyond. This trend reveals that even during times when jazz has been less popular and jazz styles less defined, many musicians remain active. It also reveals that even when a particular style of jazz dominates, musicians working within other styles continue to perform and record. For example, as fusion fell out of favor during the late 1970s, multiple musicians continued to perform bop, free jazz, Dixieland, and even fusion. The loss of a central style, however, did create a vacuum within jazz during the 1980s and 1990s that at least one group of young players would attempt to fill.

A Return to Tradition

With jazz in flux, it was perhaps surprising to many fans and critics that the next big thing showed little concern with the free jazz and fusion experiments of the 1960s and 1970s. Instead, the next wave essentially rebelled or ignored these experiments, choosing instead to return to tradition. "Around the beginning of the 1980s," writes jazz historian John Fordham, "acoustic jazz traditions neglected for close to fifteen years came triumphantly back."[81]

A number of the new African American players who favored hard bop, post-bop, and even earlier forms of jazz became known as the Young Lions. Whatever part of jazz tradition they embraced, they relied on acoustic instruments. These performers also offered a new sense of style, dressing in suits and presenting

The central figure in the Young Lions movement was trumpeter Wynton Marsalis. He has worked tirelessly on the preservation of black jazz in American culture.

Wynton Marsalis

Wynton Marsalis has been one of the most important jazz influences since the 1980s. In the following excerpt, he talks about the importance of jazz in American life:

> Jazz music has a component for every aspect of American life. Duke Ellington was from Washington [D.C.], Thelonious Monk from North Carolina, Louis Armstrong was from New Orleans, Elvin Jones is from Detroit, Fletcher Henderson was from New York, Dexter Gordon is from California, the list goes on. The great musicians come from everywhere. Charlie Parker was from Kansas City, they come from the Midwest, the North, the South, the East, the Atlantic coast, the belt. Musicians come from every direction, and they give us a portrait of the country, of just the feeling of our nation. Also, you have a depiction of all types of people. This music can be for kids. Thelonious Monk, you can play his music for children, they love it. There is the really super adult music, like some of Duke Ellington's, really mature music. And, there is the music that sounds like the Spanish contingent in the country. Jelly Roll Morton always talked about "the Spanish tinge." Then there are the versions of European music, like Duke Ellington did the *Nutcracker Suite*, and a lot of musicians do versions of European music, but it sounds like jazz. Then there's the versions of gospel music, like Horace Silver and a lot of jazz musicians in the '50s would do. There's so much.

"Wynton Marsalis," Academy of Achievement, January 8, 1999. www.achievement.org/autodoc/page/mar0int-1.

a clean image, separating themselves from the more bohemian elements of earlier jazz players. Musicians within the movement included the Marsalis brothers, trumpeter Wynton and saxophonist Bradford, trumpeters Terence Blanchard and Roy Hargrove, and saxophonist Joshua Redman.

The traditional movement of the Young Lions was not without controversy. "The resurgence of traditional mainstream acoustic jazz styles under the auspices of Wynton Marsalis would figure as the most highly publicized—and hotly contested—development in the jazz world in the 1980s and 1990s,"[82] writes jazz historian Ted Gioia. Many of the players within the movement were signed by labels early in their careers, leading, many critics believed, to the release of albums lacking a fully mature style. At the same time, many established musicians who had also continued working within more traditional forms of jazz were not given a chance to record.

One of the central players, perhaps *the* central player in this loose movement, was Wynton Marsalis. Marsalis appeared on the jazz scene during the early 1980s, first making his name as a trumpeter. "Marsalis dominated the 1980s jazz renaissance with his pearly sound, dazzling speed, and depth of knowledge,"[83] writes jazz historian Fordham. Marsalis also served as an outspoken proponent of jazz tradition as the artistic director for jazz at the Lincoln Center in New York City. In this position, he has campaigned tirelessly for the preservation of black jazz within American culture, while also offering a critical assessment of many of the innovations within jazz during the 1960s and 1970s. Both as a performer and as an educator, Marsalis has remained an active proponent of jazz musicians and jazz history.

Contemporary Jazz

During the late 1970s, when the original fusion movement had seemed to disintegrate, a new movement emerged or spun-off from jazz-rock. Contemporary jazz, commonly referred to as smooth jazz, is similar in many ways to what has been referred to as easy-listening music. Smooth jazz, like easy listening, reduces musical complications, eliminating any element that might be considered difficult or that might create discord. "It [smooth jazz] is unambiguous, non-ethnic music," writes jazz historian John F. Szwed, "generally without surprises, in which it is often difficult to distinguish one player from another."[84] Szwed also notes the tendency of early smooth jazz players to alternate between styles, sometimes playing mainstream jazz, and sometimes playing smooth jazz.

African American musicians, such as saxophonist Grover Washington Jr. and guitarist-singer George Benson, helped define smooth jazz during the 1970s and 1980s. Smooth jazz reached an even larger audience during the 1980s with the rise of white musicians, like saxophonist Kenny G. While his early albums had been considered successful, G's fourth album *Duotones* in 1986 would sell 5 million copies in the United States. A number of African Americans also reached large audiences during the 1980s

Saxophonist Grover Washington Jr. help define the smooth jazz movement of the 1980s.

and 1990s, including saxophonists Najee and George Howard. "Despite reservations from the critics," writes historian Gioia, "these musicians tended to offer the listening public well-crafted commercial product, interspersed with occasional moments of inspiration."[85]

In many ways smooth jazz has created controversy even as it has sold millions of CDs. Many critics have argued that smooth jazz players do not improvise extensively, sticking close to the melody. Some critics are also troubled by the idea that the popularity of white figures like Kenny G have perhaps overshadowed the accomplishments of African American players in the same way that bandleader and clarinetist Benny Goodman overshadowed many of his black contemporaries during the big band era. Noting the popularity of Kenny G's music, jazz instructor Mark Gridley writes, "This means, for example, that sales of just one of his [Kenny G's] albums (as many as four to seven million copies) would exceed all the recordings ever sold by Charlie Parker and John Coltrane combined."[86]

These criticisms, however, seemed to matter little to the many new fans contemporary jazz reached. "Though perceived by many musicians as more decorative than substantial," notes Gridley, "the music of Kenny G and smooth jazz defined jazz for a very large segment of American listeners during the 1980s and 1990s."[87]

Jazz Rap

During the late 1980s jazz expanded once again, combining with hip-hop to create a genre known as jazz rap. While jazz rap styles varied from one performer to the next, in general, jazz rap featured black artists exploring African roots and political consciousness against a backdrop of jazz horns and bass. Often the lyrics of jazz rap songs were spoken, not sung. Performers within jazz rap include Native Tongues Posse, the Jungle Brothers, and a Tribe Called Quest.

An early, popular example of this style was a song titled "Jazz Rap," released by Cargo in 1985. "Jazz Thing" by Gang Starr made an even stronger connection between jazz and rap with a lyric that celebrated jazz history. Within the rap, MC Guru serves as a narrator of black jazz history, reminding listeners of jazz greats from

Jazz Controversies in the 1980s

During the early 1980s, Wynton Marsalis made a number of controversial statements, criticizing other jazz musicians, including Miles Davis. Davis, however, was also critical of the attempt by Marsalis and other Young Lions to return to the past, as evident in this excerpt:

> What's he doin', messin' with the past? A player of his caliber should just wise up and realize it's over. . . . Some people, whatever is happening now, either they can't handle it or they don't want to know. They be messed up on that bogus 'nostalgia' thing. . . . That's a pitiful concept. Because it's dead, it's safe—that's what that s--- is about! Hell, no one wanted to hear us when we were playing jazz. Those days with Bird [Charlie Parker], Diz [Dizzy Gillespie], Trane [John Coltrane]—some were good, some were miserable. . . . People didn't like that stuff then. Hell, why do you think we was playing clubs? No one wanted us on prime-time TV. The music wasn't getting across, you dig! Jazz is dead.

Ian Carr. *Miles Davis: The Definitive Biography*. New York: Thunder's Mouth, 1998, p. 437.

bebop saxophonist Charlie Parker to post-bop saxophonist John Coltrane. In 1990 film director Spike Lee included the song in the movie *Mo' Better Blues*. The blending of jazz and hip-hop or rap was also expanded by sampling. In 1988 Gang Starr sampled bebop pioneer Dizzy Gillespie's "Night in Tunisia" in "Words I Manifest."

Even established jazz musicians experimented with jazz rap. In 1992 jazz trumpet innovator Davis issued his last studio album, *Doo-Bop*, an album that once again found Davis moving into new musical territory. Living in New York City at the time, Davis had wanted to record an album that reflected the sounds on the street that he heard from his apartment window. This led to a collaboration with hip-hop producer Easy Mo Bee. While the album remains transitional—Davis died before the recording was finished—it offers an auditory portrait of a style of music that—nearly a hundred years after its founding—continued to grow and flourish. In 1993 *Doo-Bop* won a Grammy Award for Best R&B Instrumental Performance.

Jazz rap has continued to develop into the twenty-first century. One of the more interesting projects has been the series *Jazzmatazz*, with the first four CD installments running from 1993 to 2007. Within the series, rapper Keith Edward Elam, known as Guru, collaborated with a number of jazz musicians including Byrd, Branford Marsalis, and Courtney Pine. These recordings reveal both the rich history and continued growth of black music within America.

The Future of Jazz

If jazz history teaches the fan, historian, and critic anything, it teaches him or her that the next big thing has never been predictable. Many New Orleans jazz musicians, for instance, were content to perform as an ensemble with little focus on the solo until Louis Armstrong came along and revolutionized the music during the 1920s. Likewise, those who performed free jazz during the mid-1960s for a small audience never expected the emergence of the more popular, electrified jazz—fusion—at the end of the decade. Jazz has thrived on unpredictable elements—the new idea, the virtuoso performer, and the after-hours jam session—and will perhaps continue to do so.

One of jazz's greatest strengths has been its ability to absorb new styles along with its ability to merge with musical forms that fall outside of jazz. While it may seem surprising to those unfamiliar with jazz, both the tradition of Armstrong and the freeness of Coleman are jazz; both the soaring vocals of Ella Fitzgerald and the open spaces of Davis's electronic music are jazz. Jazz has shown its versatility by blending with other musical styles, from classical, to South American jazz, to rock and roll. In more recent times, jazz has merged with world music, drawing and contributing to the blending of African, Asian, European, and American cultures.

Perhaps the other great strength of jazz, and one that jazz continues to exhibit in the 2000s, is its ability to celebrate and negotiate race and ethnicity. Jazz, for nearly one hundred years, has offered a showcase for African Americans to express artistry within a society that has often relegated blacks to second-class citizenship. Likewise, jazz has brought together black and white musicians, dancers, and fans, helping to close the sometimes contentious gap

Rapper Keith Edward Elam, also known as Guru, has collaborated with many jazz musicians to produce the *Jazzmatazz* series of albums.

in race relations within the United States and abroad. As a form of artistic expression that celebrates the black experience, jazz will remain a living legacy and a high watermark of American culture, the fulfillment of a quest for artistic and political freedom. Referring to the legacy of jazz, historian Alyn Shipton has written:

Of all the musical forms to emerge during the twentieth century, jazz was by far the most significant. In the early years of the century it spread first throughout the United States of America like wildfire, and then quickly to the rest of the world, where its combination of syncopation, unusual pitching, vocal tones, and raw energy touched the hearts and minds of people across the entire spectrum of social and racial backgrounds. Its message was universal, and it stood for something new, something revolutionary, something risqué that overturned the old orders of art music and folk music alike.[88]

Notes

Chapter One: The Roots of Jazz

1. John Fordham. *Jazz*. New York: Barnes and Noble, 1993, p. 12.

2. John F. Szwed. *Jazz 101: A Complete Guide to Learning and Loving Jazz.* New York: Hyperion, 2000, p. 94.

3. Geoffrey C. Ward and Ken Burns. *Jazz: A History of America's Music,* New York: Knopf, 2000, p. 4.

4. James H. Cone. *The Spirituals and the Blues: An Interpretation.* Westport, CN: Greenwood, 1972, p. 5.

5. Quoted in Willie Lee Nichols Rose, *A Documentary History of Slavery in North America.* Athens: University of Georgia, 1999, p. 515.

6. Ted Gioia. *The History of Jazz.* New York: Oxford University, 1997, p. 34.

7. Gioia, *The History of Jazz*, p. 12.

8. Ward and Burns, *Jazz*, p. 15.

9. Barry Ulanov. *A Handbook of Jazz.* New York: Viking, 1960, p. 8.

10. John Ed Hasse, ed. *Ragtime: Its History, Composers, and Music.* New York: Schirmer, 1985, p. 2.

11. Michael Erlewine, Vladimire Bognanov, Chris Woodstra, and Scott Yanow, eds. *All Music Guide to Jazz.* San Francisco: Miller Freeman, 1998, p. 1,242.

12. Lee Ostransky. *Jazz City: The Impact of Our Cities on the Development of Jazz.* Englewood Cliffs, NJ: Prentice-Hall, 1978, p. 29.

13. Ostransky, *Jazz City*, p. 30.

14. Gioia, *The History of Jazz*, p. 34.

15. Erlewine, et al., eds., *All Music Guide to Jazz*, p. 1,238.

16. Erlewine, et al., eds., *All Music Guide to Jazz*, p. 1,237.

Chapter Two: Early Jazz from New Orleans to Chicago (1900–1930)

17. Erlewine, et al., eds., *All Music Guide to Jazz*, p. 1,243.

18. Mark C. Gridley. *Jazz Styles: History and Analysis.* Upper Saddle River, NJ: Prentice Hall, 2000, p. 55.

19. Marshall W. Stearns. *The Story of Jazz.* New York: Oxford University Press, 1956, p. 161.

20. Erlewine, et al., eds., *All Music Guide to Jazz*, p. 865.

21. Stearns, *The Story of Jazz*, p. 72.

22. Szwed, *Jazz 101*, p. 104.

23. Szwed, *Jazz 101*, p. 105.

24. Mitchell Newton-Matza. *Jazz Age: People and Perspectives.* Santa Barbara, CA: ABC-CLIO, 2009, p. 97.

25. Gridley, *Jazz Styles*, p. 55.

26. Gioia, *The History of Jazz*, p. 45.

27. Gioia, *The History of Jazz*, pp. 40–41.

28. Szwed, *Jazz 101*, p. 99.

29. Gioia, *The History of Jazz*, p. 39.

30. Ostransky, *Jazz City*, p. 107.

31. Alyn Shipton. *A New History of Jazz*. New York: Continuum, 2001, p. 119.

32. Szwed, *Jazz 101*, p. 109.

33. Gioia, *The History of Jazz*, p. 60.

34. Louis Armstrong. *Louis Armstrong: In His Own Words*. New York: Oxford University Press, 1999, pp. 131–132.

35. Shipton, *A New History of Jazz*, p. 142.

36. Wynton Marsalis. "Why We Must Preserve Our Jazz Heritage." *Ebony*, February 1986, pp. 130–131.

37. Erlewine, et al., eds., *All Music Guide to Jazz*, p. 37.

Chapter Three: Harlem and the Big Band Era (1925–1946)

38. Ostransky, *Jazz City*, p. 191.

39. Gioia, *The History of Jazz*, p. 94.

40. Stearns, *The Story of Jazz*, p. 182.

41. John Leland, *Hip: The History*. New York: Harper, 2004, p. 81.

42. Gioia, *The History of Jazz*, p. 95.

43. Quoted in Gioia, *The History of Jazz*, p. 97.

44. Quoted in Shipton, *A New History of Jazz*, p. 266.

45. Gioia, *The History of Jazz*, p. 125.

46. John Edward Hass. *The Life and Genius of Duke Ellington*. New York: Simon and Schuster, 1993, p. 103.

47. Szwed, *Jazz 101*, p. 129.

48. Erlewine, et al., eds., *All Music Guide to Jazz*, p. 1,250

49. Szwed, *Jazz 101*, pp. 129–130.

50. Fordham, *Jazz,* p. 100.

51. Fordham, *Jazz*, p. 108.

Chapter Four: The Bebop Revolution and Beyond (mid-1940s–1958)

52. Fordham, *Jazz*, p. 30.

53. Fordham, *Jazz*, p. 30.

54. Gridley, *Jazz Styles*, p. 163.

55. Fordham, *Jazz*, pp. 32–33.

56. Gridley, *Jazz Styles*, p. 151.

57. Gridley, *Jazz Styles*, p. 153.

58. Martin Gayford. *The Best of Jazz: The Essential CD Guide*. San Francisco: Collins, 1993, p. 20.

59. Szwed, *Jazz 101*, p. 177.

60. Szwed, *Jazz 101*, p. 186.

61. Fordham, *Jazz*, p. 38.

62. Gridley, *Jazz Styles*, p. 207.

63. Szwed, *Jazz 101*, pp. 196–197.

64. Gridley, *Jazz Styles*, p. 156.

65. Gioia, *The History of Jazz*, p. 326.

Chapter Five: Free Jazz and Other Experiments (1959–1967)

66. Fordham, *Jazz*, p. 180.

67. Erlewine, et al., eds., *All Music Guide to Jazz*, p. 374.

68. Gayford, *The Best of Jazz*, p. 24.

69. A.B. Spellman. "Revolution in Sound." *Ebony*, August 1969, p. 88.

70. Erlewine, et al., *All Music Guide to Jazz*, p. 225.

71. Fordham, *Jazz*, p. 190.

72. Ashley Kahn. *Kind of Blue: The Making of the Miles Davis Masterpiece*. New York: Da Capo, 2000, p. 69.

73. John Fordham, *Jazz*, p. 190.

74. Erlewine, et al., eds., *All Music Guide to Jazz*, p. 1,268.

75. George Brown Tindall. *America: A Narrative History*. New York: W.W. Norton, p. 1984, p. 1,244.

76. Gioia, *The History of Jazz*, pp. 337–38.

77. Erlewine, et al., eds., *All Music Guide to Jazz*, p. 236.

Chapter Six: Fusion and Beyond (1968–Present)

78. Erlewine, et al., eds., *All Music Guide to Jazz*, p. 282.

79. Chris Smith. *101 Albums That Changed Popular Music*. New York: Oxford, 2009, p. 79.

80. Erlewine, et al., eds., *All Music Guide to Jazz*, p. 1,276.

81. Fordham, *Jazz*, p. 196.

82. Gioia, *The History of Jazz*, p. 381.

83. Fordham, *Jazz*, p. 198.

84. Szwed, *Jazz 101*, p. 264.

85. Gioia, *The History of Jazz*, p. 371.

86. Gridley, *Jazz Styles*, p. 358.

87. Gridley, *Jazz Styles*, p. 358.

88. Shipton, *A New History of Jazz*, p. 1.

For More Information

Books

Charles Alexander, ed. *Masters of Jazz Guitar*. London: Balafon, 1999. This book contains a series of essays following the development of electric and acoustic guitar within jazz. Individual essays focus on a number of great African American guitarists, including Charlie Christian and Wes Montgomery.

Bob Blumenthal. *Jazz: An Introduction to the History and Legends Behind America's Music*. New York: Harper, 2007. This title offers a readable introduction to the history and personalities of jazz, breaking down the development of jazz by covering two decades in each chapter.

John F. Fordham. *Jazz*. London: DK Adult, 1993. *Jazz* is divided into several sections, providing introductions to jazz styles, jazz instruments, and jazz biographies. Fordham also provides a timeline charting the central events of jazz's history.

Robert Gottlieb. *Reading Jazz: A Gathering of Autobiography, Reportage, and Criticism from 1919 to Now*. New York: Vintage, 1999. While many books provide the history of jazz and the biographies of jazz musicians, this book allows the musicians and critics to speak for themselves by drawing from autobiography, newspaper stories, and other sources.

Leslie Gourse. *Deep Down in Music: The Art of the Great Jazz Bassists*. Danbury, CT: Scholastic, 1998. Provides a history of the development of the bass within jazz, and emphasizes the accomplishments of a number of important players, from Jimmy Blanton with Duke Ellington to Ron Carter with Miles Davis.

Leslie Gourse. *Fancy Fretwork: The Great Jazz Guitarists*. Danbury, CT: Children's Press, 2000. Follows the development of both the acoustic and electric guitar within jazz, and highlights the innovations of players from Charlie Parker to Grant Green.

Leslie Gourse. *Sophisticated Ladies: The Great Women of Jazz*. Boston: Dutton, 2007. Provides short biographies of many women jazz singers, including portraits of African American singers Ella Fitzgerald, Sarah Vaughan, and Betty Carter.

John Edward Hasse, ed. *Jazz: The First Century*. New York: Random House, 2000. Hasse, the American music curator for the Smithsonian Institution, offers a survey of the development of jazz, accompanied by a rich display of photographs.

Billie Holiday with William Duffy. *Lady Sings the Blues*. New York: Penguin, 1956. The autobiography of jazz singer Billie Holiday, covering everything from her struggle with drug abuse to the introduction of the poignant classic "Strange Fruit."

John F. Szwed. *Jazz 101: A Complete Guide to Learning and Loving Jazz*. New York: Hyperion, 2000. Both a history of American jazz and an introduction to understanding jazz. Within the book, Szwed also provides analysis of many important jazz recordings.

Geoffrey C. Ward and Ken Burns. *Jazz: A History of America's Music*. New York: Knopf, 2002. The companion book to the Ken Burns PBS documentary. Like the film, the book contains many historical documents and a wealth of vintage photographs.

Steven Watson. *The Harlem Renaissance: Hub of African-American Culture, 1920–1930*. New York: Pantheon, 1996. Provides an introduction to the development of black culture and politics within New York City, including a survey of the jazz scene that developed within Harlem.

Audio-Video Sources

Ken Burns. *Jazz—A Film by Ken Burns*, PBS Home Video, 2001. A multi-episode history of jazz from its birth in New Orleans during the 1890s to the emergence of the Young Lions in the 1980s.

Ken Burns. *Ken Burns Jazz: The Story of American Music*, Sony, 2000. This five-CD box set offers an overview of the development of jazz from the earliest recordings in the 1910s to the rise of the Young Lions during the 1980s. The set contains ninety-four jazz tracks.

Jazz Piano: A Smithsonian Collection, Smithsonian, 1989. A four-disc collection covering piano jazz from the mid-1920s to the late 1960. Contains a booklet and sixty-eight recordings.

The Jazz Singers: 1919–1994, Smithsonian, 1998. A five-CD set covering jazz vocalists from 1919 to 1994, including Louis Armstrong, Bessie Smith, Billie Holiday, and many others.

Smithsonian Collection of Classic Jazz, Smithsonian, 1995. This five-CD box set is considered a classic overview of jazz history, and has been used by educators in the classroom. The set includes a booklet offering details on the individual jazz tracks.

Websites

Jazz Photos (www.jazzphotos.com/). Extensive photographs of jazz legends, including Billie Holiday, Dizzy Gillespie, and Charlie Parker, taken by photographer William Gottlieb.

PBS Jazz (www.pbs.org/jazz/). The PBS Jazz website is connected to Ken Burns's *Jazz* documentary and includes a Jazz Kids section with biographies of jazz greats and other information at http://pbskids.org/jazz/.

Chronology

Mid-1890s: Jazz is born in New Orleans; cornet player Buddy Bolden is believed to be the first jazz bandleader.

1905–1922: New Orleans, the birthplace of jazz, becomes the center of jazz development in the United States.

1914: W.C. Handy, known as the Father of the Blues, publishes "St. Louis Blues."

1915: Pianist/composer Jelly Roll Morton publishes the first jazz piece, "Jelly Roll Blues," in 1915.

1914–1919: Thousands of African Americans leave the South, migrating northward to New York, Chicago, and other cities.

1922: Kid Ory's Original Creole Jazz Band is the first African American band to record jazz.

1925–1928: Louis Armstrong records the *Hot Fives* and *Hot Sevens* in Chicago.

1927: Bandleader Duke Ellington opens at the Cotton Club in New York City's Harlem.

1920s and 1930s: Harlem Renaissance within New York City becomes a showcase for black poets, artists, novelists, and musicians.

1935: Big band music, also called swing, becomes the most popular music in America.

1945–1946: The birth of bebop, represented by the first recordings of trumpeter Dizzy Gillespie and saxophonist Charlie Parker.

1950s and 1960s: The rise of the civil rights movement.

1959: The release of trumpeter Miles Davis's *Kind of Blue* and saxophonist Ornette Coleman's *The Shape of Jazz to Come*.

1962: Bossa nova becomes popular; the release of saxophonist Stan Getz and guitarist Charlie Byrd's *Jazz Samba*.

1969: Jazz fusion is established; the release of Davis's *Bitches Brew*.

1980s: Smooth jazz, also known as contemporary jazz, becomes popular.

1981: Trumpeter Wynton Marsalis releases his first self-titled album.

1985: The band Cargo releases "Jazz Rap."

1988: Gang Starr samples Dizzy Gillespie's "Night in Tunisia" for "Words I Manifest."

2007: In response to the tragedy of Hurricane Katrina, trumpeter Terrence Blanchard issues the album *A Tale of God's Will*.

Index

Picture Credits

Cover: © Ted Spiegel/Corbis

© Alain De Jean/Sygma/Corbis, 89

AP Images, 84

© Bettmann/Corbis, 62

© Bettmann/CorbisArt Library, 19

Bill Spilka/Getty Images, 67

© Corbis, 59

David Refern/Getty Images, 87

© Derrick A. Thomas; Dat's Jazz/Corbis, 96

Frank Driggs Collection/Getty Images, 16, 23, 29, 64

Gai Terrell/Redferns/Getty Images, 80

George Rose/Getty Images, 91

Getty Images, 38, 40, 44, 76

Gilles Petard/Redferns/Getty Images, 51

Gjon Mili/Time and Life Pictures/Getty Images, 46

Hulton Archive/Getty Images, 11, 15, 69

Michael Ochs Archives/Getty Images, 27, 35

Redferns/Getty Images, 30, 37, 82, 100

Robert Abbott Sengstacke/Getty Images, 8, 93

Sony BMG Music Entertainment/Getty Images, 55

Time & Life Pictures/Getty Images, 49, 72

About the Author

Ronald D. Lankford Jr., a writer, editor, and independent scholar, has been writing about folk, rock, jazz, and pop for over ten years. His published works include *Folk Music USA*, concerning the American folk revival of 1958–1965, and *Women Singer-Songwriters in Rock*, published in 2010.